MUSIC THERAPY CLINICAL TRAINING MANUAL

Mary E. Boyle, Ed.D., RMT - BC
Robert Krout, Ed.D., RMT - BC

MMB

MMB MUSIC, INC.
10370 PAGE INDUSTRIAL BOULEVARD
SAINT LOUIS, MISSOURI 63132

MUSIC THERAPY CLINICAL TRAINING MANUAL

Mary E. Boyle, Ed.D., RMT-BC
Robert Krout, Ed.D., RMT-BC
State University of New York, The College at New Paltz

ISBN 0-918812-52-6

Cover Artwork: Mary Lynn Brophy
Printer: Rose Printing Company, Inc. Tallashassee, FL
3rd Printing: September, 1993
PRINTED IN U.S.A.

For a complete catalog, contact:

MMB Music, Inc.
10370 Page Industrial Boulevard
Saint Louis, Missouri 63132 (USA)

FAX: (314) 426-3590
Phone: (800) 543-3771

This manual is dedicated to our music therapy students for helping to make the system work.

Contents

IV - TREATMENT DESIGN AND MEASUREMENT

Appendix

PREFACE

This manual is designed to clarify for the student in music therapy the many decisions and tasks inherent in music therapy treatment and to aid him/her in deciding on a treatment program and carrying it out. The manual has some aspects of the "Think and Do" series which have plagued many elementary school students for years. The challenges in therapy are of the "Think and Do" variety, i.e., to develop a treatment program based on an individualized assessment of a client's strengths and needs - and to carry it out. The problems in individualizing treatment are myriad because of the many choices a therapist can make. For the novice, this may be overwhelming at times. However, we have attempted to detail certain steps toward a final treatment decision by compiling forms that ask both easy and difficult questions. (Sometimes it is not simple, though, to distinguish between an easy or a difficult question. That may depend upon both the patient and the therapist.) If you are floundering, ask for help. Asking questions can clarify for your instructor what problems you are having. Also, other students may have had an experience similar to yours that they successfully negotiated and can help you with ideas.

To gain a perspective on the actual demands of the clinical practicum, the student should read the entire manual before meeting with his/her clients each semester. Chapters focus on the main components of a comprehensive treatment program, i.e., assessment, data collection, baseline design and measurement, and treatment design and measurement. Although these are separated into chapters here, they are not separated in the therapeutic situation. The processes are interactive. The Assessment and Data Collection chapters operate in tandem as do the Assessment and Baseline Design and Measurement chapters and the Baseline Design and Measurement and Treatment Design and Measurement. This means that the student will complete work in the Assessment and Data Collection chapters simultaneously. The assessment is the basis for the development of work in both the chapters on Baseline and Treatment Design and Measurement. The manual in conjunction with your instructional sessions and/or seminars will allow you to develop appropriate treatment plans for each of your clients and support you through the process of delivering treatment.

I
ASSESSMENT

Behavioral assessment is critical to the development of effective treatment programming. Until we analyze a behavior or skill, we will not be able to increase/decrease performance of that behavior or skill. This chapter is designed to help you conduct behavioral assessments of music skills and nonmusic skills which are often the focus of music therapy sessions. The goals of assessment procedures are to evaluate client proficiency or functioning level in terms of potential growth and to interest and involve the client in music therapy. (Translation: We want the client to attend the session.)

In order to evaluate areas for potential growth, we must also analyze what the demands of a given task are. Behavioral assessment is specific to a given task. This means that you must think of possibilities for programming for your client in broad terms and then develop your own assessment procedure composed of the subskills necessary to perform a given behavior. What does it take to play a harmonica? How many fingers do you really need to play the guitar? (Ask Leo Fender - or behaviorally assess your client's functioning level and guitar types.)

This chapter is divided into three parts: The Initial Interview, Assessment Procedures, and Charting for Assessment Information. The initial interview is critical to identification in broad terms of what the client enjoys musically and where you will need to develop assessment procedures to examine the present abilities of the client. The assessment procedures are a refinement of these in terms of task demands and client skills. Charting is your contract with the client concerning the focus of music therapy.

Initial Interview

The Initial Interview with your client is meant to serve two purposes: To give your client a positive impression of music therapy and his/her therapist (you) and to give you basic information about your client, e.g., his strengths, weaknesses, preferences, presenting problem, prior treatments, and basic biographical information. Depending upon the facility, there will be varying time spans for the initial interview. You will have at least twenty minutes for which you should plan. You may ask yourself, "Twenty, minutes, how can I talk for that long?" That's not the idea. Let the client do the talking, signing, or pointing to a communication board! You do the asking and waiting (while smiling). . . .

Prior to meeting with your client you should ask the person making the referral certain questions. What is the client's presenting problem? How does he/she see music therapy in the client's overall program? What behaviors would he/she like to be the focus of therapy (in terms of music and nonmusic behaviors)? Obtain a general description of the highest priority problem and then request appropriate additional information. Ask if the client is on special medication. Complete the physical checklist if the client is in a hospital setting. Ask about prior treatment.

In order to get a good description of the presenting problem, ask behavior analysis questions concerning the antecedents, behaviors, and consequences. Ask questions about frequencies, durations, and settings for the problem behaviors. Antecedents can relate to settings, type of prompts, words spoken, etc. This will depend upon the targeted behavior. These questions will help you determine settings and materials for your assessment sessions to follow.

Your next question may be, "Well, what do I ask my client?" Let's not rush - let's think about what our goals are for an initial interview. We need to make the client comfortable with us (so that he/she will return) and obtain basic information on the client's physical appearance, general behaviors, e.g., eye contact, facial expression, social interaction - verbal and nonverbal, setting of observation, any noticeable deficits or disabilities, stated referral reason. This means that we focus not only on the questions we ask, but the client's responses - verbal and nonverbal.

There are some basic procedures in interviewing that it is good to review. Iwata, Wong, Riordan, Dorsey, and Lau (1982) identified interviewing behaviors for psychology students at Johns Hopkins Hospital. These have been adapted for music therapists.

1. Greet the client by name.
2. Give your name and affiliation.
3. Give a brief description of music therapy applicable to the population of which the client is a member.
4. Tell the client what you are going to do today, e.g., take pertinent biographical information and treatment information, complete a preference checklist, observe motor abilities for instrument performance, test number identification, etc. Prioritize the activities. (This does not mean that if you are checking "reality orientation" you say to the client, "I am checking to see if you are oriented to reality" or "I need to make sure if you know where you are." Say instead, "I need to just get some basic information that I'll jot down so that when I leave I'll be sure to remember.")
5. Explain each of the procedures from 4 to the client.
6. In closing, tell the client what you learned from the above and that you will be back <u>(when)</u> to consider <u>(options)</u>. At that time, both of you will write a contract for music therapy services. Say good-bye and escort the client to an appropriate location. At some facilities, it will be possible to do an assessment in conjunction with the initial interview.

The above procedures are meant for both verbal and nonverbal clients. Many times we treat a nonverbal client who can communicate as if we were nonverbal. June Bigge (1982) has some very helpful hints for communicating with people who cannot talk to us. These are:

1. Find and use signals for "yes," "no," "I don't know," "sometimes," and "maybe."
2. Find out what other signals a child uses.

3. Provide opportunity for initiative in communication.
4. Ask questions one at a time.
5. Avoid giving unintentional clues.
6. Accept only clear signals.
7. Allow time for expression of ideas.
8. Narrow the options to find the category about which the person has something to say.
9. Continue conversations until expressed messages, ideas, feelings, or attitudes are clarified (for as long as the discussions seem worthwhile).
10. Talk "up to" not "down to" disabled individuals.
11. Recognize deadlocks.
12. Teach the child's associates what works.

Reading through these you may be thinking how difficult many of them are, e.g., number 6, "Accept only clear signals." You're right! However, there are diplomatic ways of doing this. These are especially important in an initial interview. Take the onus on yourself and say, "I am afraid I did not understand that last phrase," or "Was that question a bit on the ambiguous side?" In desperation, a smile can get you out of many communication deadlocks. There are many common situations which when you are on the spot for a question in "yes/no" terms it is difficult to solve, June Bigge (1982) suggests:

1. The problem may be a physical one. A question such as, "Are you comfortable?" will tap that problem.
2. The problem may be that the therapist or client is locked into one idea. A statement such as, "Let me think this over to see if I can come back next week with some other questions. Will you do the same?" may alleviate that problem.
3. The initial interview is meant to help us get to know one another and be more comfortable - a difficult goal - so a little "down to earth" honesty may help. Tell the client, "I am in need of a little help here and I hope you're willing to stick it out with me."

Charting Your Initial Interview

A record of all therapy sessions must be kept in the patient's chart. At the initial interview stage, the therapist merely notes the session.

Sample (handwritten in BLACK ink)

Date: Music Therapy Note

Time: Met with Pt as per referral. Will conduct assessment on ____(dates)____.

-- *I.M.A. Therapist, MTS*

(Signature) (Credentials)

Initial Interview Data Form

Client Name ____ Age __________

Placement ____

List any noticeable deficits the client might exhibit in the following areas:

Speech:

Hearing:

Display of Eye Contact:

Fine Motor Coordination:

Gross Motor Coordination:

Following Instructions:

Attention Span:

Other:

General Description of Presenting Problem:

Client Music Activities Preferences:

Areas of Focus for Assessment and Rationales:

Assessment

As music therapists, we work in two major settings, one-to-one (individual) and group. In both of these cases, it is necessary to design treatment programming on an individual basis. We need to assess each person's strengths and deficit areas and then design a program incorporating these. In music, it is definitely to our advantage to maximize the client's strengths in order to minimize his/her weaknesses.

Assessment should be conducted in both group and individual settings to analyze how the client interacts in social and individual situations. In the case of the individual targeted for one-to-one programming, we may observe quite different behaviors with the client in group and individual settings.

Assessment in an Individual Setting.

When we assess clients in a one-to-one setting, the first order of business is setting the client at ease. In order to do this, you need to have your materials ready and explain briefly to the client what both of you are going to do. For example, last week Alginon said he used to play harmonica. You have brought two harmonicas in the same key and your data collection materials. You might say, "Alginon, I brought a harmonica so that we can play together. Do you remember the names of any songs you used to play? You can't play? Well, you know what they say about riding a bicycle. Do you remember *Down in the Valley*? No? Well, that's about my level so let's start there . . ." (If we believed clients' verbal reports or negative/self deprecatory statements, we'd never get started, e.g., listen to yourself as you attempt to explain to your practicum supervisor, "There's no way I can . . ." As an instructor who has had to listen to these litanies, I can only say, "Poor, poor pitiful me.")

Your assessment data sheet should list behaviors targeted for assessment from your initial interview. Examine your client preference form, the reason given for the referral, interview information, and construct an assessment based on those. The following is merely a sketch of what you need to develop.

Client's name:

Time(s) and Setting(s):

Definition of Behaviors to be Examined (strengths and deficits):

At this point, you may have only a general idea of the behaviors. If so, leave space to write in further information.

Procedure: How are you going to analyze these behaviors? Be specific so you can remember what you mean to do. If you are going to ask questions or give verbal directions, write them out.

Results: What can the client do now? Or What is he doing now? Give measurements of the behaviors. Describe conditions under which the behaviors occurred, e.g., partially/fully prompted. Describe the consequences of the behaviors in terms of the therapist and client. (Sometimes patients smile when they hear themselves; others may cry.) Leave space for specific comments or requests, e.g., the way he played the guitar - Third Hand Capo, right fingers got stuck in the strings, or repertoire.

Assessment in a Group Setting

When we assess clients in a group situation we are often part of that group, not a mere observer. Your first response may be "I can't. I've got to play the B^b Major chord for Ernie's song request - it's my first barre - and I can't remember the words so I have to look at the sheet music - and I have this great ostinato for the drums, but it's a little tricky to do it right - and YOU'RE GOING TO BE WATCHING ME SING - and I don't really know the song - it's only been a week since I first heard of it and I spent all last Saturday running around trying to find it and . . ." "Hold your Horses!" Let's back up and begin at the beginning. We are here to increase/decrease certain client behaviors, not therapist perseveration. We need to look at the client and listen to him/her so that we can decide what is appropriate to change.

There are certain social behaviors we expect in a group situation: appropriate eye contact, smiling/appropriate affect, greeting/acknowledgment of other group members who are familiar, conversation among peers, physical posturing and proximity appropriate to conversation, etc. There are other behaviors that are undesirable, e.g., staring into space, no conversation with peers, self-stimulation, bizarre or negative verbal/vocal behaviors, attempts to leave the group, temper tantrums and physical isolation from the group.

There are also desirable group music behaviors involved in performing one's part with the group. For example, keeping the beat, maintaining the ostinato/part assigned, singing/playing correct pitch, and improvising when appropriate are all behaviors we want to maintain or increase.

Make up a data sheet that will allow you to gather data appropriate for your specific clients. An example follows on page 10; remember that's all it is. Don't write down categories on which you cannot collect data, e.g., number of seconds smiling (screaming may be a relatively easy matter). After your initial session, decide in what areas you want to focus for the next session. Make a new assessment chart listing those behaviors that you want to measure/examine. Remember that both antecedents and consequences affect the behavior. You may need to analyze the behavior in different settings. Where and when does your client disrobe? Did the client begin disrobing when you were introduced? What was your reaction and that of the staff. (Is the client still assigned to music therapy?)

In addition to examining antecedents and consequences, don't forget to examine the behavior. Think of how it is best analyzed by initially defining/describing it. Then consider whether you want to time it or count it. Does the client always perform it in the same way? Or, does he try many ways to do it?

Assessment of certain behaviors requires you to meet individually with a client for a few minutes, e.g., motor behaviors necessary for instrumental performance. Is it realistic for Sunshine to attempt dulcimer given her diagnosis of hemiplegia - right side? (It may be fine; you won't know until she tries it in a non-threatening situation.) In other cases, medications may drastically affect a client's coordination. The client may have played guitar prior to hospitalization and be unaware of decreased capacities. He/she may become extremely anxious when confronted with a task no longer performed well. It is important to be aware of any medications the client is taking which may affect his/her behaviors. Check the most recent *Physicians' Desk Reference* in your library. In other cases, the client's disability may affect affective behavior related to task demands, e.g., a person who has had a recent stroke (CVA-cerebrovascular accident) may begin crying suddenly. Reassure the patient as you continue with the assessment.

Diplomacy is essential in assessment situations. Don't be afraid to praise the client's efforts and/or reassure them about his/her performance. "This is only the beginning . . ."

Sample Group Assessment Data Sheet

Psycho-Geriatric Group

Client Name	Greets Therapist (GT)/Greets Peers (GP)	Orients to Therapist (OT)/to Peers (OP)	Sings w/Group ( ) for each occurrence	Keeps on Beat, Rhythm Instruments (+/-)	Maintains Assigned Part (+/-)	Appropriate Eye Contact (+/-)	Appropriate Verbalization (+/-)	Requests Specific Songs (Name)	Bizarre or Negative Verbalization	Other
1.										
2.										
3.										
4.										
5.										
6.										
7.										

Courtesy: Diane Gillman

Sample Second Session Assessment

Rhythm Instrument Behavior Checklist

Date:																		
Client Initials:																		
Behavior:																		
1. Comes to group when directed																		
2. Sits in designated space when directed																		
3. Stands in designated space when directed																		
4. Leaves group area when directed																		
5. Verbally responds to offer of instrument																		
6. Approximates name of instrument verbally*																		
7. Correctly names instrument*																		
8. Picks up instrument/apparati when directed																		
9. Holds instrument when directed																		
10. Plays instrument																		
11. Plays instrument as directed with other: ( )																		
12. Grasps mallet when directed																		
13. Ceases playing instrument when directed																		
14. Puts down instrument when directed																		
15. Hands instrument to therapist when directed																		
16. Hands instrument to peer when directed																		
17. Other:																		
18. Other:																		
19. Other:																		
20. Other:																		
21. Other:																		

* **Instruments used:** ______________________________

____

Prompt code: A = without assistance, B = verbal prompts, C = physical prompts,
D = manipulation (putting through), O = no performance, NA = not applicable

Name ______________________ **School** ______________________

Sample Second Assessment Session

Singing Group Behavior Checklist

Date:																		
Client Initials:																		
1. Comes to group when directed																		
2. Sits in designated space when directed																		
3. Stands in designated space when directed																		
4. Leaves group when directed																		
5. Remains quiet when directed																		
6. Remains quiet while others are singing																		
7. Improves posture when directed																		
8. Sings when directed																		
9. Makes eye-contact with therapist when directed																		
10. Knows and can sing 1 song from memory																		
11. Knows and can sing 2 songs from memory																		
12. Knows and can sing 3 songs from memory																		
13. Sits close to peer without touching peer																		
14. Stands close to peer without touching peer																		
15. Praises peer once per session																		
16. Selects songs from group to sing when invited																		
17. Other:																		
18. Other:																		

Prompt code: A = without assistance, B = verbal prompts, C = physical prompts,
D = manipulation (putting through), O = no performance, NA = not applicable

Name ______________________________ **School** ______________________________

Charting for Assessment Information

Congratulations! You have completed your assessments of music and nonmusic behaviors and identified areas for therapy. You are now ready to chart your Music Therapy Initial Assessment.

The Initial Assessment is the basis for delivery of services to the client. In it, you state your assessment findings in terms of the data you recorded and the goals and rationale for services to be delivered. The goals are defined further by stating initial behavioral objectives that can be tested during baseline. This document is essentially a contract between the therapist and the client defining the services to be delivered. The therapist is then accountable for them.

There is a standard form used by all therapists for initial assessments. This may vary slightly from facility to facility. However, the information is necessary regardless of format. Assessments and evaluations are always typed, as they are forwarded upon request to other facilities if the patient is transferred.

The writing style of the assessment should be succinct and informative. Information is of primary importance; inferences regarding data are secondary or unimportant. The topic sentences of your first paragraph should contain a description of the client, e.g., Patient (Pt) is a 7-y-o Caucasian female diagnosed as autistic-like. This is to make sure that each therapist/teacher/physician/nurse is talking about the same client. The body of the first paragraph contains information regarding the assessments - dates, length of sessions, and findings. The second paragraph states your goals and the rationales for them in terms of your assessment findings. It concludes with specific behavioral objectives for a defined period of time. Because we write these objectives prior to conducting baseline and treatment, there is a high probability that they will need to be modified. Despite this, objectives are a standard part of initial assessments as they provide direction for behavior change. (Be sure to review the sections on writing behavioral objectives in the next chapter.)

The following is a sample of charting for a Music Therapy Initial Assessment.

Initial Music Therapy Assessment

Patient (Pt) is a 7-y-o Caucasian female diagnosed as autistic-like. Music therapy assessment was conducted on 9/10, 9/11, and 9/12 in forty five minute sessions. Pt was referred to music therapy because of her interest in music, i.e., tantrums when her SONY Walkman is removed. Pt was observed in both classroom and music room settings. In the classroom, Pt sat by herself for forty-five minutes on two days; on the second day, she walked to the listening center and put on her SONY Walkman and returned to sit alone at her desk. She exhibited a finger-flicking movement near her right ear for twenty minutes on the first day and twelve minutes the second. In the music room on the third day, she ran from instrument to instrument playing them carefully. She allowed the therapist to physically guide her hand on a xylophone pattern for three minutes. Although she does not verbalize, she exhibited a broad range of communicative behaviors for expressing what she wanted, e.g., took therapist's hand, gazed at objects, did not move from desired object, tantrummed for ten seconds when drum was removed. She grasped mallets appropriately for Orff work.

Goals for the first three months include responding to peer-initiated social interactions in the music room and performing simple rhythmic and instrumental melodic ostinati to traditional first-grade repertoire, e.g., *Sesame Street* songs, American folk literature. As the Pt demonstrated that she enjoys music and it can be a social setting demanding social interactions, it is recommended that she have another patient with her at her sessions. This would allow training for the patient to look/listen for another peer as they play music together. The introduction of age-appropriate music literature allows her a normalizing educational experience.

Behavioral objectives for the next three months are:

1. When Pt 2 passes an instrument to client, she will take the instrument and look at her within three seconds, four out of five times per session.
2. When Pt 2 nods to Pt to begin her ostinati, she will begin on the next beat each time.
3. When Pt 2 reaches to take Pt's hand for a circle song, she will reach out and take the hand within three seconds.
4. When the therapist sings/plays songs such as *I Love Trash*, *Go Tell Aunt Rhody* and *The Old Gray Cat Is Sleeping*, Pt will accompany with specified varied rhythm patterns of steady beats in duple and triple meters.
5. Given the same conditions as above, Pt will play 3-4 tone ostinati keeping a steady beat through one verse.

____

Signature, MTS

In addition to the typed assessment, you should chart each session under the category, "Progress Notes." (Look for the tab in chart marked "Progress Notes.") Three sentences are adequate until assessment is finalized.

II
DATA COLLECTION

Why Data?

Collecting data on client performance is an integral aspect of accountable music therapy practices and procedures. In fact, methods of careful measurement and subsequent evaluation are critical to many treatment programs which incorporate applied behavior analysis techniques. By having a working expertise with such methods, the clinical music therapist is at an advantage in making positive contributions to treatment teams composed of many professionals, including psychiatrists, psychologists, teachers, speech therapists, occupational and physical therapists, nursing personnel, and others.

Effective means of measuring client progress benefit everyone involved, including the client, therapist, facility, and society. The client gains by being involved in a treatment program geared specifically to his/her unique strengths and weaknesses. As we all learn skills at our own rates, a treatment course which can react and adapt to subtle changes in performance will be one which can be tailored for maximum learning. The therapist benefits by receiving feedback on his/her own performance as a therapist in the form of identifiable improvements in client skill acquisition and overall functioning. Music therapists often work with behaviors that are difficult and challenging to manage and teach. Feedback on client performance, therefore, can be an indicator to the therapist that he/she is indeed making an impact on the client's life. The facility profits by having one more professional contributing to the welfare of its clients in a thoughtful and qualified manner. A treatment center is only as successful as the strides made by its clients in their various endeavors to learn and be happy. Finally, society benefits by the improved life situations of one or a few of its members.

Pinpointing

When targeting a skill or behavior for training or modification, the therapy student must describe that skill in clearly observable terms. From the initial interview and subsequent assessment, the student will have arrived at a goal for the client to meet during treatment, and a rationale for why that goal is important and reasonable. Goals are broad measures of targeted improvement. They are usually comprised of separate skills that the client learns, either sequentially or simultaneously, to meet the goal.

In order to accurately assess and teach these skills, the student therapist must pinpoint, or operationally define, the various behaviors that combine to form the skills. Questions regarding the skills and the subskills which are involved must be answered before an appropriate data collection method can be implemented.

To go through this pinpointing process, answer the questions on the form on page 27. After you have completed the form, have a friend read your behavioral descriptions, and then tell you exactly what the client will be expected to do to meet the goal. If there is any information lost in the relating, redo the form until another reader clearly understands what you are describing. A client's success will depend on how he/she relates to his/her environment, which is made up of many people and events. If your goal, behaviors and subskills are ambiguous, then your client may not realize success, even if the goal you set is met.

Writing Behavioral Objectives

A behavioral objective allows the therapist to design consistent assessment and teaching situations which can help the client learn in an organized manner. A behavioral objective includes three components: a condition, a behavior, and a criterion (Wheeler & Fox, 1972). Two behavioral objectives will be written by the student therapist for each of the two subskills identified for assessment first on the Pinpointing Worksheet. One will be a pre-baseline objective, and one will be a post-baseline objective. The difference between the two will be that after gathering baseline data, a final target level of performance will be included as an aspect of the criterion.

The pre-baseline objective will include:

1. Condition: Under what conditions the client will be expected to perform the behavior. This will include any verbal or nonverbal directive given the client by the therapist, a description of where the client is expected to perform the behavior, and any materials or other relevant information that sets up the circumstances for the client to demonstrate the skill/subskill.
2. Behavior: This is a description of exactly what the client is expected to do. Only observable actions should be included.
3. Criterion: How well, or at what level of independence, the skill will be performed. Any aspect of the performance of the behavior that will make it more apparent that it has or has not been performed correctly can be included in the criterion section.

These three components will be combined into a single, readable sentence written so that it places the condition first, followed by the behavior, and finally the criterion. The objective should leave nothing to the imagination of the reader or an impartial observer.

Task Analysis

A task analysis, as its name implies, involves a careful examination of the requisite behaviors necessary to perform a given task or skill at a specified proficiency level. The component behaviors are listed sequentially. The final task analysis lists behavioral objectives including the condition, behavior, and criteria for accomplishment of a skill.

Following this analysis, the therapist or teacher can decide how to teach the skill. The therapist/ teacher may decide that each behavioral objective must be met before proceeding to the next objective in the sequence. He/she may decide to guide the student through several behavioral objectives with graded levels of independence, guidance, prompting, or proficiency. Certain procedures, such as backward chaining, involve guiding the student through initial levels and requiring independence at a final behavior.

Task Analysis Worksheet

What are the key behaviors in sequence necessary for proficient performance of the desired music skill or nonmusic skill?

1.

2.

3.

4.

5.

etc.

In this continuum, where do you place your client? ____________________

____

____

Design a task analysis incorporating behavioral objectives sequentially for each key music and nonmusic behavior you listed from page 7.

Music/Nonmusic Goal: ____________________

____

Task Analysis:

TASK ANALYSIS OF COURTEOUS SELECTION OF PARTNERS

Behavioral Instructional Objectives

Condition	Behavior	Criteria
1. Given a record with spooky sounds and the verbal direction, "I am your phantom partner, sit on the floor facing me."*	The students will sit on the floor facing the therapist.	Within ten seconds, students will be one foot apart.
2. Given the verbal directions, "Mirror, Mirror, on the wall/Show these humans one and all/With the phantom to rise or fall."	Students will watch closely and make the same simple motions as the phantom.	Within five seconds of a motion change.
(Optional) 3. Given the verbal directions, "Mirror, mirror on the wall/Quiet shall come or all will fall," and the quiet cue of an index finger near the lips.	The students will not speak or make loud noises.	Within five seconds.
4. Given the verbal directions, "The phantom must leave now, _______ will be the new phantom," and the therapist's cue to come forward.	The named child will come to front of group and sit, then make a simple motion.	Within thirty seconds.
5. Same as above.	Other students will make same motions as the new phantom.	Within five seconds of a motion change.
6. Given the verbal directions, "Mirror, mirror, on the wall/Cast a spell on one and all/Tell each human silently to find a partner/Within three counts/ Or from the grave the phantom will arise/To choose new partners for one and all."	Each child will find a partner.	With no sounds above a whisper within three counts.
7. Given the verbal direction, "_______, ________, ________, ________, are phantoms; ________, ________, ________ are mirrors; make a head/ hand/etc. movement to the music."	The children will make the named movement according to their parts.	Within fifteen seconds performing assigned parts.

* The spooky record should continue throughout the "Phantom" activity.

Condition	Behavior	Criteria
8. Same as above with role switch.		
9. Given the verbal directions, "Partners, partners - separate, a new one find while I wait. By the count of three/ Or the phantom you will see."	The children will each find a new partner.	By the count of three.
10. Same as 7		
11. Given the verbal directions, "Phantoms, phantoms, one must not touch/Or to dust one will turn."	Any child touching his partner will stop.	Within five seconds.

Throughout the year, the activities will vary for finding a partner. If isolates mutually develop, group contingencies for activities will be established. If isolates are continuously alone and refuse to join others, then individual contingencies of popular music listening could be instated.

SAMPLE TASK ANALYSIS OF PLAYING I AND V7 ON THE HARMONICA

(Six Year Old Nonverbal Autistic Child)

Behavioral Instructional Objectives

Condition	Behavior	Criteria	Reinforcement Contingency
1. After being told by the therapist to "Sit in the chair."	The child will sit in the chair facing the therapist with her feet on the floor, her hands in her lap and her buttocks in contact with the seat of the chair.	For ten seconds on 16 out of 20 consecutive trials.	For proper sitting in each trial, the child will receive a bite of her favorite food and verbal and/or physical approval.*
2. After being told by the therapist to "Sit in the chair" and "Look at me."	The child will bring both eyes to meet the gaze of the therapist and sustain this contact.**	For four seconds while sitting properly on 16 out of 20 consecutive trials.	For proper looking on each trial -- same as above.
3. After being told by the therapist to "Sit in the chair," "Look at me," and "Do this." (Therapist models hand claps.)	The child will clap hands.**	Within five seconds while sitting properly and after looking at the therapist on 16 out of 20 consecutive trials.	For proper clapping on each trial -- same as above.
4. After being told by the therapist to "Sit in the chair," "Look at me." and "Do this," (Therapist models raising arm over her head.)	The child will raise her arm over her head.**	Within five seconds while sitting properly and after looking at the therapist on 16 out of 20 consecutive trials.	For proper raising of arm on each trial -- same as above.
5. After being told by the therapist to "Sit in the chair," "Look at me," and "Do this." (Therapist models stamping foot on floor.)	The child will stamp her foot on the floor.	Within five seconds while sitting properly and after looking at the therapist on 7 out of 10 consecutive trials.	For proper foot stamping on each trial, the child will receive a bite of her favorite food and verbal and/or physical approval.
6. Same as above, except therapist models blowing out big breath.	The child will blow out big breath.	Same as above.	For proper breath blowing on each trial, the child will be allowed to blow once with the therapist into a "Bubble Magic" wand.
7. Same as above, except therapist models picking up and putting back on the table a harmonica.	The child will pick up and put back on the table a harmonica.	Same as above.	For proper picking up and putting down of harmonica -- same as "Bubble Magic" above (includes verbal and/or physical approval).

*Verbal approvals would consist of remarks similar to: "Good Girl," "Excellent sitting or looking," "I like the way you're clapping, sitting." Physical approvals would be similar to: knee rubs, shoulder pats, arm rub.

** Technically, the behaviors are cumulative for sitting and looking and then the new behavior. This presentation has been simplified to only list the new behavior.

Condition	Behavior	Criteria	Reinforcement Contingency
8. Same as above, except therapist models standing up.	The child will stand up.	Same as above.	For proper standing up on each trial, the child will receive a bite of lunch or food and physical and/or verbal approval.
9. Same as above, except therapist models sucking in air and gradually letting it out.	The child will suck air in and gradually let it out.	Beginning within five seconds while sitting properly and after looking at the therapist on 7 out 10 consecutive trials.	For proper sucking in and letting air out on each trial, the child will receive one sip of soda or favorite juice through a straw in a glass
10. Same as above, except therapist models touching cheek with hand.	The child will touch her cheek with her hand.	Within five seconds while sitting properly and after looking at the therapist on 7 out of 10 consecutive trials.	For proper touching of her cheek, the child will receive a bite of lunch or favorite food and verbal and/or physical approval.
11. After being told by the therapist to "Sit in the chair," "Look at me," and "Do this." (Therapist models touching toe with her hand.)	The child will touch her toe with her hand.	Within five seconds before and after sitting properly and looking at the therapist on 7 out of 10 consecutive trials.	For proper toe touching on each trial, the child will re-ceive a bite of lunch or her favorite food and verbal approval.
12. Same as above, except therapist models putting harmonica to mouth and then putting it down.	The child will put har-monica to mouth correctly and put itdown on the table.	Within five seconds while sitting properly and after looking at therapist on 7 out of 10 consecutive trials.	For proper handling of the harmonica on each trial, the child will be allowed to blow once in the "Bubble Magic Wand" and receive verbal and/or physical approval.
Items 3 - 12 are to be repeated in order twice at each session until a criterion of 7 out of 10 on four successive sets is reached.			
13. After being told by the therapist to "Sit in the chair," "Look at me," and "Look here." (Thera-pist points to a book on the table between them.)	The child will focus her eyes on the book.	Within five seconds and for at least four seconds on 16 out of 20 consecutive trials	For proper focusing on each trial, the child will receive a bite of lunch or favorite food and verbal and/or physical approval.
14. Same as above, except therapist points to the harmonica on the table.	The child will focus her eyes on the harmonica.	Same as above.	For proper focusing on each trial -- same as above.
15. Same as above, except therapist points to a comic of a big face blowing out air.	The child will focus her eyes on the comic face blowing out air.	Same as above.	For proper focusing on each trial, the child will be allowed to blow once in the "Bubble Magic Wand" and receive verbal and/or physical approval.

Condition	Behavior	Criteria	Reinforcement Contingency
16. After being told by the therapist to "Sit in the chair," "Look at me," and "Look here." (Therapist points to comic of face sucking in air.)	The child will focus her eyes on the comic face sucking in air.	Within five seconds and for at least four seconds on 16 out of 20 consecutive trials.	For proper focusing on each trial, the child will receive one sip of soda or favorite juice through a straw in a glass and verbal and/or physical approval.
Items 13 - 16 are to be alternated in a random order until the child reaches a criterion of 16 out of 20 trials.			
17. After being told by the therapist to "Sit in the chair," "Look at me," and "Point to the book."	The child will point (extend the index finger and curl thumb and other fingers) to the book.	Within five seconds on 16 out of 20 consecutive trials.	For proper pointing to the book, the child will receive a bite of lunch or favorite food and verbal and/or physical approval.
18. Same as above, except therapist says, "Point to the harmonica."	The child will point to the harmonica.	Same as above.	For proper pointing to the harmonica--same as above.
19. Same as above, except therapist says, "Point to the harmonica."	The child will point to the face blowing air.	Same as above.	For proper pointing to the face blowing air on each trial, the child will be allowed to blow once in the "Bubble Magic Wand" and receive verbal and/or physical approval.
Items 17 - 19 are to be alternated in a random order until the child reaches a criterion of 16 out of 20 on two consecutive sessions.			
20. Given two faces, one sucking and one blowing and directions from the therapist to "Point to the face blowing air."	The child will point to the face blowing air.	Within five seconds on 7 out of 10 consecutive trials.	For proper pointing on each trial, the child will be allowed to blow once in the "Bubble Magic Wand" and receive verbal and/or physical approval.
21. Same as above, except therapist says "Point to the face sucking air."	The child will point to the face sucking air.	Same as above.	For proper pointing on each trial, the child will receive one sip of soda or favorite juice through a straw in a glass and verbal and/or physical approval.
Items 20 and 21 are to be alternated randomly until a criterion of 16 out of 20 has been reached in two consecutive sessions.			

Condition	Behavior	Criteria	Reinforcement Contingency
22. Given the verbal instructions to suck or blow air.	The child will suck or blow air as directed.	Within five seconds on 16 out of 20 consecutive trials	For proper sucking, the child will receive a sip of soda or juice. For the proper blowing, the child will be allowed to blow in the "Bubble Magic Wand" once for each trial. In both instances, the child will receive verbal and/or physical approval.
23. Given the verbal instruction to "Put the harmonica to your mouth and then put it back on the table."	The child will put the harmonica to her mouth and then put it back on the table.	Same as above.	For properly putting the harmonica to her mouth and back on the table, the child will receive a bite of lunch or her favorite food and verbal and/or physical approval.
24. Given the verbal directions to "Pick up the harmonica and blow into it." (This will make a I chord.)	The child will pick up the harmonica and blow into it.	The therapist will be able to hear the I chord within five seconds on 16 out of 20 consecutive trials.	The therapist will sing *The Farmer in the Dell* for each correct trial. Note: If this is not reinforcing, go back to the "Bubble Magic Wand." In both instances there will be verbal and/or physical approval.
25. Given the verbal directions by the therapist to "Put down the harmonica."	The child will put down the harmonica on the table.	Within five seconds on 16 out of 20 consecutive trials.	For properly putting the harmonica down, the child will receive lunch or favorite food bite for each trial and verbal and/or physical approval.
Items 24 and 25 are to be alternated in order for each trial.			
26. Given the verbal directions by the therapist to "Pick up the harmonica and suck air from it." (This will make the V^7 chord.)	The child will pick up the harmonica and suck air from it.	The therapist will be able to hear the V^7 chord within five seconds on 16 out of 20 consecutive trials.	For properly sucking air from the harmonica, the child will receive a sip of soda or juice through a straw from a glass and verbal and/or physical approval.
27. Given the verbal directions by the therapist to "Put down the harmonica."	The child will put down the harmonica on the table.	Within five seconds on 16 out of 20 consecutive trials.	For properly putting the harmonica down, the child will receive lunch or favorite food bite for each trial and verbal and/or physical approval.
Items 26 and 27 are to be alternated in order for each trial.			

HALF PRICE BOOKS®

Half Price Books
1835 Forms Drive
Carrollton, TX 75006
OFS OrderID 39528690

Thank you for your order, Main Address!

Thank you for shopping with Half Price Books! Please contact service97@hpb.com. if you have any questions, comments or concerns about your order (113-4973066-5930648)

Visit our stores to sell your books, music, movies games for cash.

SKU	ISBN/UPC	Title & Author/Artist	Shelf ID	Qty	OrderSKU
S469580455	9780918812520	Music Therapy Clinical Training Manual Krout, Robert M.,Boyle, Robert Ellis	SH&P 2.4	1	

SHIPPED STANDARD TO:
Main Address
800 Avondale Ave
1033841-1-0311
Grandview Heights OH 43212
zypxchqnwm9p8bz@marketplace.amazon.com

ORDER# **113-4973066-5930648**
AmazonMarketplaceUS

Condition	Behavior	Criteria	Reinforcement Contingency
28. Given the verbal directions of the therapist to "Blow" or "Suck" and the pointing directions of the therapist to the correct comic face and a harmonica.	The child will blow or suck on the harmonica as directed.	A correct I or V^7 chord will be heard by the therapist within five seconds on 16 out of 20 consecutive trials.	The therapist will sing *Down in the Valley* or *Lou, Lou, Skip to My Lou* as the correct chords are played. Therapist will sing only if correct chord is played. The child will receive verbal and/or physical approval for correct responses.
29. As the therapist points to the correct comic face for blowing or sucking.	The child will blow or suck on the harmonica.	A simple song, e.g., *Down in the Valley* or *Lou, Lou,* will be correctly accompanied by the child.	The therapist will sing the song as it is played, stopping only if a chord is incorrect. The child will receive verbal and/or physical approval for correct responses.

Choosing a Data Collection Procedure

Data concerning client performance are usually recorded using fairly straightforward observation techniques. Data represent client behavior, so the system of observation and measurement must be accurate. It is easy to decide on a system that does not really measure what you think it should. Such a mistake will make any conclusions about client performance suspect at best.

At this point, you have broken down your goal into music and nonmusic skills. You have also broken down those skills into subskills and prioritized them. The next steps are to decide what dimensions of the subskills are of concern, and then choose a data collection system that measures those dimensions. To do this, answer the questions on the following form. Do not gloss over a question just because the behaviors you are interested in seem easy to measure in a particular way. Different clients display similar behaviors differently and it is up to you to detect and be sensitive to those differences.

Designing a Data Collection Sheet

During each session that you meet with or observe your client, you will have to actually collect and record your data in the manner you have decided upon. To make this process workable, you will need to have ready and waiting a data collection form that you can use with minimum confusion. You will probably be the one running the session **and** recording data, so be prepared to actually use this form. The following information will be necessary.

1. A space for your name.
2. A space for your client's name. **NOTE!!** If you are conducting a group session, design one form that can be used for the session. This will mean a separate area for each client's data on the form. During a session is not the time to start rummaging around to find someone's form.
3. A space for the time of the start of the session.
4. A space for the time of the conclusion of the session.
5. A space for the date.
6. A space for the name of the facility.
7. A space for the name of the observer, and if the observer is for reliability.
8. A space for a description of the target behavior pinpoint.
9. A code for how the behavior is being judged (+ for correct, - for incorrect, P for prompted, etc.).
10. A section with space to record the raw data (number of occurrences, amount of time in seconds, etc.).
11. A space for a summary of that session's behavior (rate, percentage).
12. Other spaces as needed for your situation. You may find it useful to have a space for recording any unusual events that occurred during the session, or a space for any comments.

Data Collection Worksheet

Student therapist ________________________ Client ________________________

Facility ________________________ Date ________________________

1. The music subskill that I will be measuring first is: ________________________

____

The nonmusic subskill that I will be measuring first is: ________________________

____

2. The property of the music subskill that I am most interested in is:

frequency____ duration____ latency____ topography____ setting____

The property of the nonmusic subskill that I am most interested in is:

frequency____ duration____ latency____ topography____ setting____

3. This property of the music subskill, ________________, will be best expressed as:

raw data____ rate____ percentage____ other ________________

This property of the nonmusic subskill, ________________, will be best expressed as:

raw data____ rate____ percentage____ other ________________

4. The equipment needed to record the ________________ of the music subskill is:

counter____ stopwatch____ two stopwatches____ cassette____ recorder____

video recorder____ other ________________________

The equipment needed to record the ________________ of the nonmusic subskill is:

counter____ stopwatch____ two stopwatches____ cassette____ recorder____

video recorder____ other ________________________

5. The person collecting music data will be ________________________

The person collecting nonmusic data will be ________________________

6. Music data will be collected continuously____ or intermittently____

Nonmusic data will be collected continuously____ or intermittently____

Note: If you are measuring more than one music and/or nonmusic behavior, answer the above questions for each additional behavior.

Actually Using Your Daily Data Collection Sheets

Now that you have designed a data form, you must actually use it on a regular (every session) basis. Here are some areas to address for easier data collection. Go through them one by one, and check off the items that you have obtained, practiced and addressed.

1. I have put the following materials together into a "field kit":

____clipboard for holding data sheets together

____data sheets (make plenty of extra copies)

____a pencil and pen each with clips, attached to the clipboard

____stopwatch(es)

____watch with second hand

____wrist or pencil counter if necessary

____video recorder

____graph paper

____cassette recorder

____other

2. I have practiced using my data forms with the following friends:

________________________________ on ____________________
name date

________________________________ on ____________________
name date

3. During the client sessions I will keep my data sheets ____________________
actual location

____________________, and I or ____________________
name of observer

will record data at ________________________________
when during the session

by ________________________________
what will actually be recorded on the data sheet

4. The most difficult aspect of recording data will be ____________________

____

Entering Daily Data on a Summary Data Sheet

To get an idea of how your client is performing over time, you will need to enter the data you collect each session onto a record that reflects ongoing performance. This sheet must feature:

1. A space for your name.
2. A space for your client's name. **NOTE!!** Unlike the daily data sheet, you do not need to include all your clients on this cumulative record sheet. You have written a goal for an individual client,

and this sheet will reflect progress made towards that goal. You will also be able to transfer daily data onto this form immediately after the session, so you will not be as rushed.

3. A space for the name of the facility.
4. A space for the description of the target behavior pinpoint.
5. Spaces for date entries corresponding to the sessions to be held.
6. A space for entering the daily data from each session that corresponds to each date entry. Be sure to identify the form that the data is to take.
7. A space above the date entries to mark if the data is baseline or treatment.

Reminders

- Be sure that the way you represent each day's data is consistent. Do not change from raw frequency to rate or duration in the middle of your program.
- If a client is absent for a session, make sure you record the date and the fact that you did not meet with the client. Do not simply go on with the next date space without noting the absence.
- Transfer daily data totals (means, etc.) immediately after the session is over.

The following Sample Data Forms are to be used as models. Do not photocopy them. Design your own.

Music Therapy Frequency Recording Raw Data Sheet

Date: ______________________________ Facility: ______________________________

Therapist: ______________________________ Observer: ______________________________

Length of session in minutes: ______________

Client: ______________________________

Behavior pinpoint: ____

____

Frequency (record each occurrence as a /):

____

Number per minute (total number/total time): ______________________________ = rate

Client: ______________________________

Behavior pinpoint: ____

____

Frequency (record each occurrence as a /):

____

Number per minute (total number/total time): ______________________________ = rate

Client: ______________________________

Behavior pinpoint: ____

____

Frequency (record each occurrence as a /):

____

Number per minute (total number/total time): ______________________________ = rate

Client: ______________________________

Behavior pinpoint: ____

____

Frequency (record each occurrence as a /):

____

Number per minute (total number/total time): ______________________________ = rate

Assessment-Duration Recording

Client ______________________ Therapist ______________________

Setting ______________________ Group ______________________ Date ______________

Behavior Pinpoint ____

____

Session	Total Duration of Session	Total Duration of Pinpoint	% of Session that Pinpoint Occured
1			
2			
3			
4			
5			
6			
7			
8			
9			
10			
11			
12			
13			
14			
15			
16			
17			
18			
19			
20			

Multiply Handicapped Music Therapy

Date ________________________________ Therapist ________________________________

1. **Client** - number of words of chorus in *The Gambler* sung understandably:

   _______/43 = _______%

2. **Client** points to picture of song within five seconds when verbally directed:

   Country Roads ____ Railroad ____ Sunshine ____ Puff ____ Hammer ____

3. **Client** lowers head to touch chest within five seconds of verbal directive:

   Trials 1) _____ 2) _____ 3) _____ 4) _____ : _____% performed

4. **Client** vocalizes in *I've Been Working on the Railroad* on cue "M sing!" within five seconds.

   Trials 1) _____ 2) _____ 3) _____ 4) _____ : _____% performed

5. **Client** looks at therapist within three seconds of directive "Name, look at me."

   Trials 1) _____ 2) _____ 3) _____ 4) _____ 5) _____ : _____% performed

Discrete Trial Training Data Collection Form

Therapist ______________________________ Facility ______________________________

Client ______________________________

SESSIONS — indicate date and if session is B (baseline) or T (treatment)

TRIAL	1	2	3	4	5	6	7	8	9	10	11	12	13	14	15	16	17	18	19	20
1																				
2																				
3																				
4																				
5																				
6																				
7																				
8																				
9																				
10																				
11																				
12																				
13																				
14																				
15																				
16																				
17																				
18																				
19																				
20																				
TOTAL																				

+ = occurrence   o = nonoccurrence

Prompt Level (if appropriate): I = independent, G = gestural, P = physical, M = manipulated,
NB = no occurrence of behavior

Definition of Target Behavior:

Reinforcer: (include contingencies)

Response Interval _____ seconds   Inter-trial Interval _____ seconds

Music Therapy Time-Sampling Raw Data Sheet

Date______________________________ Facility______________________________

Therapist____________________________ Observer____________________________

Behavior Pinpoint ____

____

Mark + for occurrence and o for non-occurrence of pinpoint at end of interval.

Client	___m,	___m,	___m,	___m,	___m,	___m,	___m,	___m,	% of + intervals

Typing Data Chart

DATE ______________ TRAINER ___________ OBS ___________

Body Position:

Wheelchair _________

Bed _______________

Time of Day:

Began_______________________________

Ended_______________________________

TRAINING: (Character Order) (I = Independent, PG = Physically Guided)

1. ________	I PG	5. ________	I PG	9. ________	I PG	13. ________	I PG
2. ________	I PG	6. ________	I PG	10. ________	I PG	14. ________	I PG
3. ________	I PG	7. ________	I PG	11. ________	I PG	15. ________	I PG
4. ________	I PG	8. ________	I PG	12. ________	I PG	16. ________	I PG

Comments ____

____

TESTING: (Character Order, Condition, and Results)

		COR	A/PG	INC			COR	A/PG	INC
1. _______	NC C/I M				16. _______	NC C/I M			
2. _______	NC C/I M				17. _______	NC C/I M			
3. _______	NC C/I M				18. _______	NC C/I M			
4. _______	NC C/I M				19. _______	NC C/I M			
5. _______	NC C/I M				20. _______	NC C/I M			
6. _______	NC C/I M				21. _______	NC C/I M			
7. _______	NC C/I M				22. _______	NC C/I M			
8. _______	NC C/I M				23. _______	NC C/I M			
9. _______	NC C/I M				24. _______	NC C/I M			
10. _______	NC C/I M				25. _______	NC C/I M			
11. _______	NC C/I M				26. _______	NC C/I M			
12. _______	NC C/I M				27. _______	NC C/I M			
13. _______	NC C/I M				28. _______	NC C/I M			
14. _______	NC C/I M				29. _______	NC C/I M			
15. _______	NC C/I M				30. _______	NC C/I M			

TOTALS: No Comment: Cor ______ A/PG ______ Inc ______

Comment of Correct or Indication of Key when Incorrect:

Cor ______ A/PG ______ Inc ______

Music w/Comment or Indication: Cor ______ A/PG ______ Inc ______

*A/PG = Attempted/Physically Guided

Individual Assessment Data Sheet

Date: O = did not recognize or pronounced incorrectly

Client:

Alphabet: A B C D E F G H I J K L M
N O P Q R S T U V W X Y Z /26

Numbers: 1 2 3 4 5 6 7 8 9 10 /10

Colors: Red Blue Green Purple Yellow Brown
Pink Orange White Black /10

Pronunciation of Vowels:

ă ā

ĕ ē

ĭ ī

ŏ o

u ū

Pronunciation of Consonants:

b-bat
c-cat ch-chalk
d-dog
f-fish
g-girl & gym
h-hill
j-jump
k-kite

l-look
m-milk
n-nest
p-pretty ph-phone
r-red
t-tap th-through
q-quick
s-sister

v-vest
w-water
x-xylophone & extra
y-yellow
z-zebra

Rhythms:
Slow: 2/2, 3/4, 4/4 Fast: 2/2, 3/4, 4/4

Courtesy: Renee Falanga

Therapist: ______________________________

Client: ______________________________

Date: ______________________________

WALKING

To Session ______________ From Session: ______________

NON-COMPLIANCE

trials	+/-
1	______
2	______
3	______
4	______
5	______
6	______
7	______
8	______
9	______
10	______
11	______
12	______
13	______
14	______
15	______
16	______
17	______
18	______
19	______
20	______

Number of CORRECT RESPONSES

1	
2	
3	
4	
5	
6	
7	
8	
9	
10	

Total of correct responses: ______________

Length of session: ______________

Rate (correct responses per minute) : ________

Courtesy: William Brodginski

III
BASELINE DESIGN AND MEASUREMENT

Obtaining a Baseline

By this point, you have identified the strengths and weaknesses of your client, targeted a goal, selected and prioritized behavior pinpoints, and written behavioral objectives to begin measurement in both music and nonmusic areas. The next step is to obtain a pre-treatment, or baseline measurement of the client's level of functioning in each of the two skill areas. By accurately measuring where the client is now, you can (1) predict where the client would be if you did not begin a treatment program, (2) have data to give you a realistic idea of how much the client might learn in the course of the therapy program, and (3) have a source of comparison between now and later in terms of whether or not your client is learning.

In actually conducting baseline measurements, you want to make sure that all environmental conditions are kept the same. You want to get a reliable indication of the client's behavior with as few outside sources of variability as possible. It is also important to remember that the observation procedures you implement in baseline will be the same ones you use during treatment. Do not make the mistake of changing the way you test the client or measure and record data when you institute treatment. If your data collection procedures don't work during baseline, change them.

What you will be looking for in the baseline data is some indication of the client's true skill level. This will be reflected in the graph as a slope in either an ascending or descending direction (trend) or the absence of a slope (steady state). Baseline data should be collected for three sessions, assuming that a true picture of the client's behavior can be obtained. Excessive data variability means that more careful observation is necessary (translation: more sessions).

Baseline Procedure Worksheet

Student Therapist ______________________________ Client ______________________________

Facility ______________________________ Date ______________________________

1. The music subskill(s) to be observed during baseline will be ______________________________

   ____

2. Data will be collected by ______________________________ using the following procedure
   (name)
   (describe exactly how the client will be observed, and how the data will be actually recorded): _____

   ____

   ____

   ____

3. During baseline, the client will be reinforced for ______________________________
   (specific behaviors)
   by me ______________________________
   (specific reinforcement techniques)

4. Data collection will begin on ____________________
   (date)

5. The nonmusic subskill(s) to be observed during baseline will be ______________________________

   ____

6. Data will be collected by ______________________________ using the following procedure
   (name)
   (describe exactly how the client will be observed, and how the data will be actually recorded): _____

   ____

   ____

   ____

7. During baseline, the client will be reinforced for ______________________________
   (specific behaviors)
   by me ______________________________
   (specific reinforcement techniques)

8. Data collection will begin on ____________________
   (date)

Graphing and Inspecting Baseline Data

Collecting data during baseline and treatment conditions allows the therapist to visually assess a client's performance. It is very difficult to look at raw figures on a data collection sheet and determine what is happening in terms of behavior change.

What you want to be able to assess from your baseline data is the client's level of functioning prior to your treatment program. To construct a graph which can help you in your assessment, follow these steps:

1. Plot an ordinate (vertical axis) and an abscissa (horizontal axis). Be sure to leave room to the left of the ordinate and below the abscissa for labeling your axes.
2. Label your ordinate with the system that you have chosen to represent client performance (frequency, duration, etc.). Make sure to raise your zero point above the point where the abscissa and ordinate intersect. Mark your ordinate in gradations which can accurately represent the actual level of performance. You should be able to read the actual level directly from the graph. Make the label next to the ordinate as clear and concise as possible (e.g., number of negative statements per minute).
3. Label your abscissa for time passage (sessions, days, etc.). Make sure you label enough sessions to represent the number of times you plan to meet with your client.
4. Label the graph at the bottom of the page, in a space that will not interfere with plotted data points. You will have two graphs, one for the music behavior and one for the nonmusic behavior.
5. Plot your data points after each baseline session. Connect the points with a solid line. When your connected points suggest a trend or steady state, draw a solid vertical line between the last baseline data point and the place on the abscissa that is for the next (treatment) data point. Label your initial phase BASELINE in the middle of and above your data points.
6. Compute a mean level of baseline performance as you proceed. Total the performance figures, and divide by the number of elapsed sessions. When you have completed your baseline, plot the mean on your graph with a horizontal dotted line.

Graphing and Inspecting Treatment Data

Data on client performance during treatment will give you an indication of the effectiveness of your program. Clinical decisions to change your procedures will be based in part on interpretation of treatment outcomes. In order to gain such information from your graph(s), continue plotting data following these guidelines:

1. Plot your first treatment data point. Do not connect this with the previous data point from baseline. Continue to plot and connect treatment data points as described for baseline plotting procedures.

2. Label your treatment phase in the middle of and above your data points. The label should reflect the nature of your treatment procedures, for example, "CONTINGENT SONG CHOICE" or "SUNG INSTRUCTIONS."
3. If you implement a new phase, such as a return-to-baseline or a different treatment procedure (as in an alternating treatments design), be sure to follow the above instructions for each phase.
4. Mean levels of treatment performance can help you determine changes in level amid variability in the data. Means for treatment(s) can be figures and plotted as in baseline.

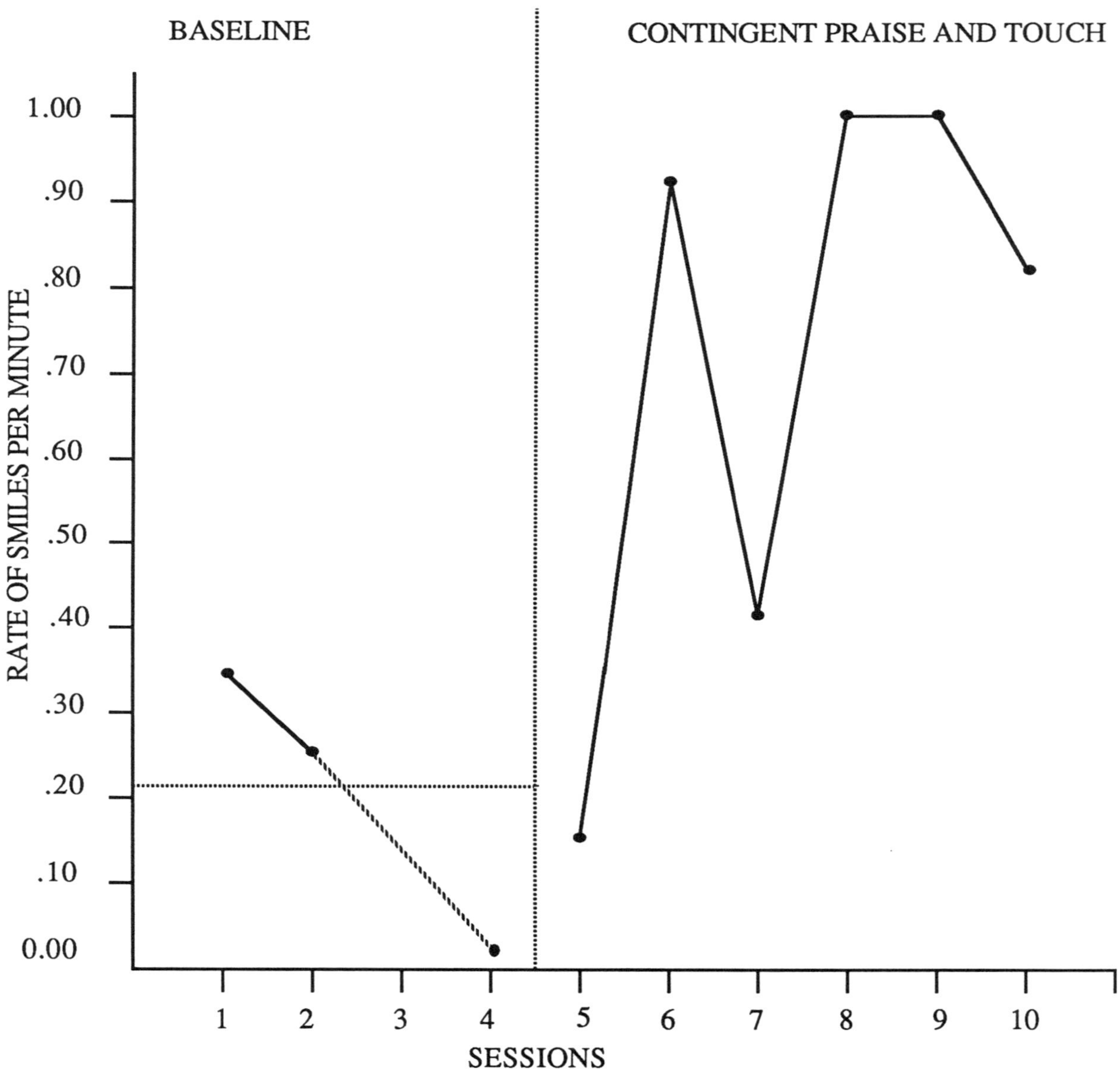

Courtesy: Robyn Hurwitz

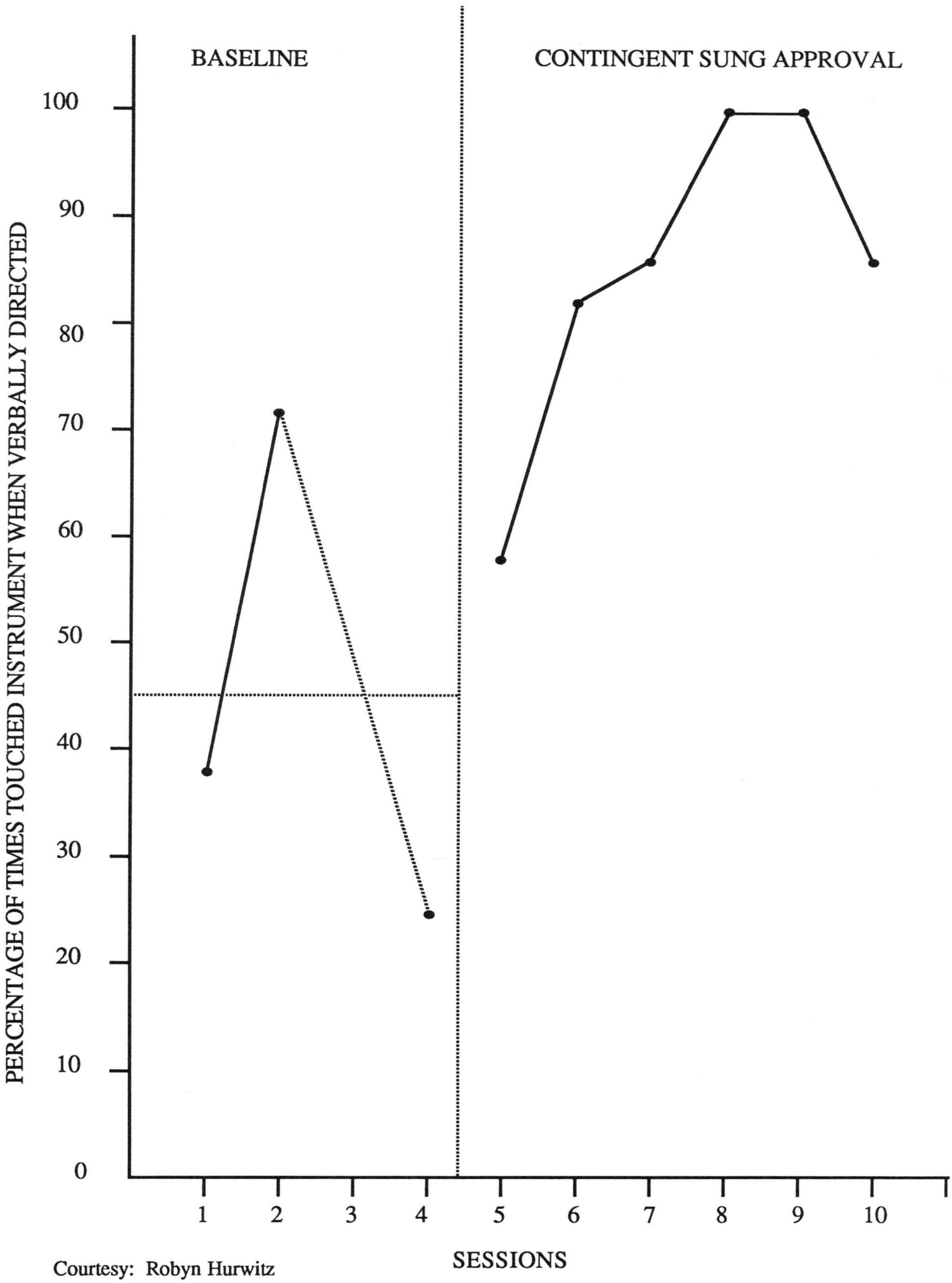

Courtesy: Robyn Hurwitz

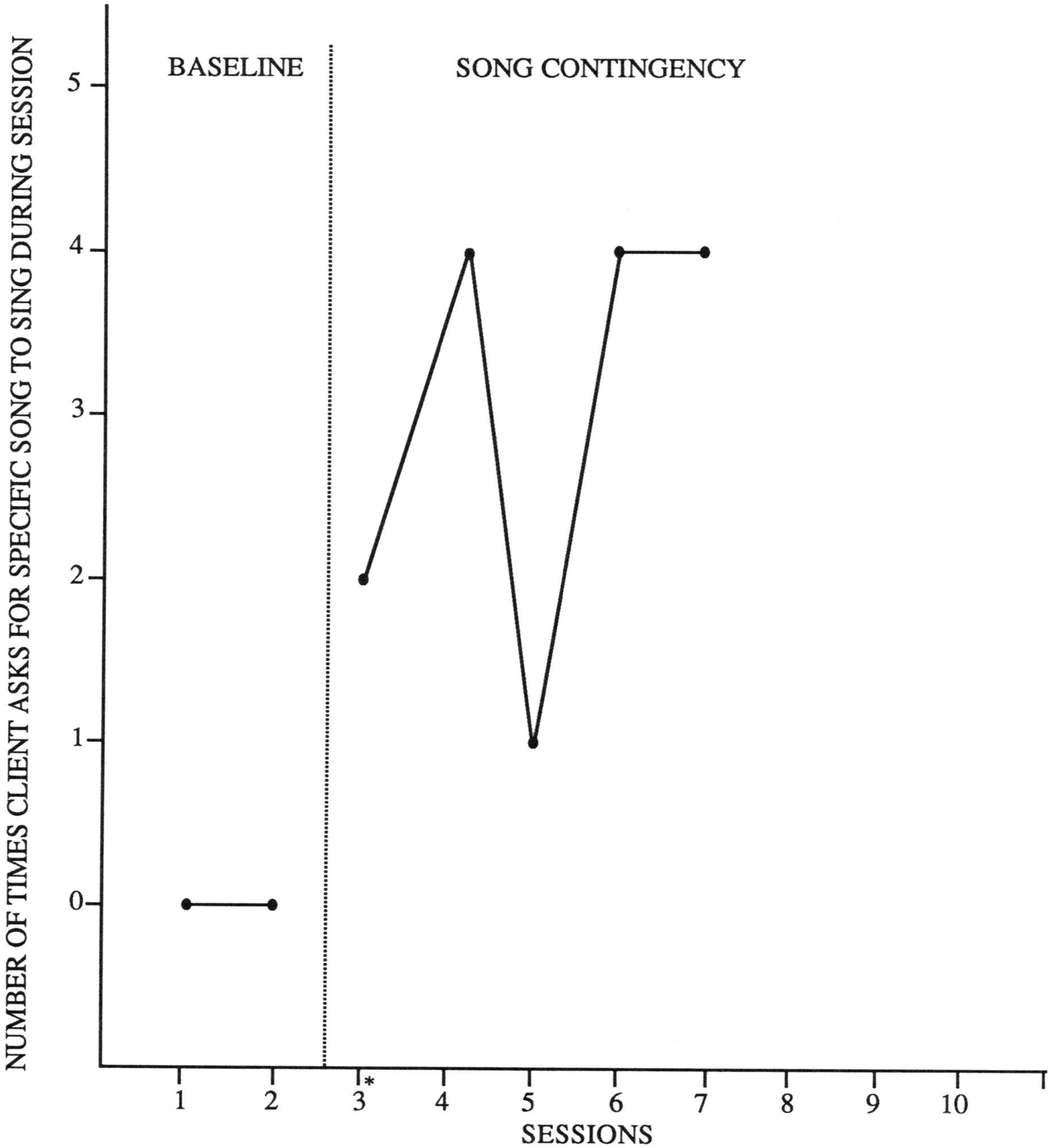

* Client missed two sessions between sessions 3 and 4

Courtesy: Jeanne McPartland

Charting During Baseline

So far, you have written chart notes regarding your initial and follow-up meetings with your client. Basically, your baseline chart notes should reflect the nature of your interaction. As with all charting, you should be precise and to the point. Remember, your chart notes are official reflections of your work. They should be written so they can be read easily, understood immediately, and reflect your status as a professional. Your baseline chart notes should include:

1. Date and time (24-hour clock) of the entry.
2. Chart note identification: e.g., "Music therapy note."
3. A sentence stating that you have begun (or are continuing) baseline measurement of ____(the actual target behavior of your client)________.
4. A sentence describing your client's level of performance for the session.
5. A summary sentence which may include a non-data observation of the client's behavior (general behavior in the session, etc.) or any other pertinent information.
6. Your signature (legible) and title (music therapy student), with a co-signature (MT-BC) if necessary.

Things to Remember

1. Chart only in black ink.
2. Do not leave any blank spaces in the note which could be tampered with.
3. Chart immediately after you finish meeting with your client.
4. Do not mention another client by name, only as "peer" or "group member."

Keep your chart notes together, and in a cumulative record. This will approximate a facility's procedures. If your facility has special charting procedures, have a staff member explain them to you.

Charting may seem like busywork, but a client's chart is his/her "life record." Improper or negligent charting can erase gains made in a therapy program. Charts are taken very seriously and are legal documents.

Targeting a Final Criterion Level of Performance for the Behavioral Objective

You have now collected baseline data for three sessions and should have a fairly clear picture of your client's skill level in each of the two areas of measurement (music and nonmusic). If your data have been extremely variable, you should continue to observe your client. Sometimes client behavior is extremely variable and may appear even more so if you only observe the client once a week. You might also need to re-evaluate your data collection procedures. They could account for variability in the data.

When you do have a stable baseline, or one that indicates a definite trend, you are ready to set a target level of performance for the criterion section of your behavioral objective. As it stands now, your objective includes a statement of how well the behavior will be performed, or at what level of independence.

Including this criterion was necessary so you could measure exactly how the client performed on that skill during baseline. Now that you have that information, you can set a level of performance that you will help the client reach during the treatment phase(s) of your program. Knowing exactly how high to set a criterion is difficult, but you can follow some guidelines:

1. The objective should be reachable. Do not set a criterion level that seems impossible. A standard level is often "80% correct." Very few things need to be done perfectly.
2. The objective should not be so easy that it will be met in a day or a week. You should expect your client to meet the objective in three to four months.
3. The objective must take into account the individual learning patterns of your client. From your observation and information, determine if your client is a fast, medium, or slow learner. Talk to teachers and other staff people, or talk to the client for assistance in this.

Post-Baseline (Treatment) Behavioral Objective Worksheet

Student Therapist ______________________________ Client ______________________________

Facility ____ Date ________________________________

1. The pre-baseline music objective reads ____

   ____

   ____

2. The mean baseline performance on the music subskill was ____________________________

3. I think that the client can reach ______________________________ on the music subskill
   (frequency)

4. The music behavioral objective with this final target frequency now reads ________________

   ____

5. The pre-baseline nonmusic objective reads ____

   ____

   ____

6. The mean baseline performance on the nonmusic subskill was __________________________

7. I think that the client can reach ______________________________ on the nonmusic subskill
   (frequency)

8. The nonmusic behavioral objective with this final target frequency now reads _____________

   ____

* This procedure must be employed in determining criteria for all objectives in the task analysis.

Obtaining Reliability Data

Problems develop in data collection when two or more people don't agree on what actually happened in the session. Even though they might be using identical data collection sheets, they may have interpreted the client's behavior differently. To help identify these potential problems, you can do "reliability checks" periodically. This process consists of having your observations compared with those of another student, teacher or other staff person. In your situation, have your peer observer be the reliability person during their peer observations. This should be done once during baseline, and once during treatment. Follow these steps:

1. Have another person observe your client and collect data. Make sure that they understand exactly what you are measuring and that they have been trained by use to use the data form. It is not important that they understand your treatment program, or exactly what music therapy is, etc. Make sure that their data form is marked "Reliability."
2. Calculate reliability using this formula:

$$\frac{\text{number of agreements}}{\text{number of agreements plus disagreements}} \times 100 = \text{interobserver reliability}$$

3. If your reliability quotient is 90% or above, you're in good shape. If it is below 90%, talk with your observer and try to figure out the problem. Keep a record of your checks below.

Interobserver Reliability

Baseline: My data total _____________, My reliability observer's total ____________.

Reliability quotient = ____% on ___(date)____.

Treatment: My data total _____________, My reliability observer's total ____________.

Reliability quotient = ____% on ___(date)____.

IV
TREATMENT DESIGN AND MEASUREMENT

Treatment

"Treatment," the moment you've been waiting for! Now, for your razzle-dazzle remedy. Where to begin is the question.

Outline a specific treatment variable or treatment package. How is treatment going to differ from baseline? What are you keeping the same? (Your baseline was your treatment? Problems . . .) Develop a procedure that can account for client improvement in terms of the behavior targeted for change. After all, when you treat a patient and he/she improves you need to chart this information and report it at rounds. Have a rationale for your procedure. Ask yourself, "How closely related is the treatment I am contemplating to the behavior I am measuring?" "Why do I think this will work - desperation? or anticipation?" "Cosmic" treatments, e.g., sensory integration procedures, patterning, etc., cannot be related to a specific behavior. Think of possibilities where you will be able to measure treatment change within six to eight weeks (the time you have with your client).

Learning is the goal of therapy. Ask yourself, "How can I help my client learn _____?" There are a few basics to good teaching, i.e., model the desired behavior, verbally/physically prompt the behavior initially, let the client try it him/herself, and REINFORCE successive approximations, REINFORCE correct responses, and REINFORCE time spent trying hard. (How did you learn to play your instrument?)

The simplest treatment variable, such as reinforcing the client for correct responses or looking away from your client when he/she is not on task, is often the most effective treatment. There are other times when it is necessary to design a treatment package. The only problem with a treatment package is that we do not know the effects or lack thereof of any component of the package, e.g., we may not need to physically **and** verbally prompt the answers. A partial verbal prompt with reinforcement may be adequate and result in greater independence.

There is an excellent series of "how-to" books on treatment for nonmusic behaviors such as self-stimulation and maladaptive behaviors. Topics covered include: negotiating a behavioral contract, using sensory extinction, reducing autistic and severely maladaptive behaviors, and treating self-injurious behaviors. These are published by Pro-Ed of Austin, Texas. They may give you some ideas if you have difficulty deciding what to do with your client.

Write out and practice what you are going to say and do during treatment. Then practice with a friend. If you are physically guiding a client on a motor behavior, you may not have a hand free to activate a tape recorder for reinforcement. (No, you don't need to eliminate the reinforcement from your treatment. That's why we have feet and foot pedals.)

Within a few sessions after you begin treatment, you should notice some behavior changes on your graphs. Many times we notice a phenomenon called "extinction burst." This refers to an increase in rate of a behavior which in some case we are trying to decrease. (This also occurs in reversal designs during the second baseline.) Other changes are positive, an increase in a desired behavior. If you do not notice changes, ask yourself if you are actually applying your treatment variable. Frequently, we think we are doing something which we are not. Often, we do not apply our treatment because we have not practiced it enough, e.g., planned ignoring, reinforcing a client every fifteen seconds. If this is not the problem, then it is good to examine your behavioral objective. Can the client meet the proficiency aspect of the criterion? How often? Are the conditions adequate to elicit the desired response? (We may be pointing to the correct answer with an autistic child for whom extra-stimulus prompts are distractors.) Is the prompt an adequate cue? Are we inadvertently changing the conditions by giving different directions and expecting the same behavior? Is the behavior defined adequately? Have I changed my definition in effect?

After you have carefully considered those questions, you are ready to consider other treatment problems. These necessitate returning to your original behavior analysis in the assessment section. Re-examine your analysis in terms of the "A, B, C's" of behavior, the antecedents, behavior(s) and consequences. (What IS happening during the therapy session and outside of it?) What factor(s) that I noted in my assessment have I forgotten? What have I noticed since my assessment? Re-examine the targeted behaviors as you did during your assessment period. Write up your new analysis and begin again with your new baseline. While you're conducting the baseline, design a new treatment program. (Cliché for the Day: If at first you don't succeed . . .)

If you really feel that you need just one little change (in the itty-bitty category), you may be able to rationalize this with an ABB_1AB_1 design. (Don't let yourself get caught in the B to infinity pit. Therapists are paid to have perspective on the problem, not obsession/perseveration with their "treatments.")

Treatment Procedure Worksheet

Student Therapist ______________________________ Client ________________________________

Facility _______________________________________ Date __________________________________

1. The music subskill to be observed during treatment is ______________________________________

____

2. Data will be collected by ________________________________ using the following procedure (describe exactly how the client will be observed, and how the data will be actually recorded). Beginning on ____
(date)

____

____

____

3. During treatment, the client will be reinforced for __________________________________
(specific behaviors)

by me ____
(specific reinforcement techniques)

4. The nonmusic subskill to be observed during treatment will be ______________________________

____

5. Data will be collected by ________________________________ using the following procedure (describe exactly how the client will be observed, and how the data will be actually recorded). Beginning on ____
(date)

____

____

____

____

6. During treatment, the client will be reinforced for ___________________________________
(specific behaviors)

____

by me ____
(specific reinforcement techniques)

____

____

Treatment Effectiveness Worksheet

Student Therapist ______________________________ Client ______________________________

Facility ______________________________ Date ______________________________

1. The music behavioral objective reads ______________________________

____

2. Describe your graph on client music behaviors. (Does it show a rising/declining slope in the desired direction? Is there a change in slope between baseline and treatment? Does your graph show a change in level between baseline and treatment? Was there stability in baseline and treatment?)

____

____

____

____

3. Troubleshooting areas: What level of proficiency did the client reach on the music behavior? (A. Did the client meet the performance proficiency criterion of the behavior in individual trials? How often? B. If not, should the criterion or condition of the behavioral objective be changed? Why? C. Did the client meet the numerical criterion for performance for the session? D. Was there instability? Can it be accounted for in terms of other occurrences in the client's day? [e.g., doctor's examination, cold, vomiting, etc.])

____

____

____

____

____

____

4. What suggestions would you have for a person continuing your treatment of the same individual? Were you able to apply your treatment procedure as originally conceived?

____

____

____

5. The nonmusic behavioral objective reads ______________________________

____

6. Describe your graph on client nonmusic behaviors. (Does it show a rising/declining slope in the desired direction? Is there a change in slope between baseline and treatment? Does your graph show a change in level between baseline and treatment? Was there stability in baseline and treatment?)

____

____

____

____

7. Troubleshooting areas: What level of proficiency did the client reach on the nonmusic behavior? (A. Did the client meet the performance proficiency criterion of the behavior in individual trials? How often? B. If not, should the criterion or condition of the behavioral objective be changed? Why? C. Did the client meet the numerical criterion for performance for the session? D. Was there instability? Can it be accounted for in terms of other occurrences in the client's day? [e.g., doctor's examination, cold, vomiting, etc.])

____

____

____

____

____

____

____

8. What suggestions would you have for a person continuing your treatment of the same individual? Were you able to apply your treatment procedure as originally conceived?

____

____

____

9. Any additional thoughts/comments?

____

____

Charting Treatment Information

There are two types of information to be charted related to treatment, Progress Notes and the Final Assessment. The Progress Notes are charted as in baseline with the addition of information on treatment, e.g., "Treatment of ___(procedure)___ was instituted on ___(date)___. Pt scored ___(number)___ of ___(number)___ on ___(behavior)___. This is an increase/decrease of ___(number)___ from ___(number)___ during baseline." (Comments regarding Pt response can also be added regarding adaptations, style, etc.)

The Final Assessment is similar in some aspects to the Initial Assessment. It is typed and filed in the Evaluations/Assessments section of the patient's chart. The first paragraph gives the patient description, initial goals and baseline data. The second paragraph includes a description of treatment procedures and data on patient performance in terms of assessment and baseline objectives. It concludes with recommendations concerning future programming. (Information from the Treatment Effectiveness Worksheet can be incorporated into this assessment.) A second style for the Final Assessment is to include in the first paragraph information regarding patient description and initial goals. One can then give comparative data between baseline and treatment regarding response ranges, means, modes, slopes, and/or levels. For example, "During baseline, Pt moved his fingers within 10 secs. for a mean of 1/10 and a range of 0-3/10. During treatment of fifteen secs. of contingent music, Pt had a mean of 6/10 responses and a range of 0-10/10." The second paragraph involves recommendations for future programming.

Sample Termination Assessment

Patient is a 17-y-o Caucasian female diagnosed as severely mentally retarded. The behaviors that we included in treatment were walking, non-compliance and matching numerals. At the beginning of treatment, S. walked to the session in two minutes and forty-five seconds. At the end of treatment, S. walked to the session in one minute and fifty-seven seconds. At the beginning of treatment, S. walked from the session in one minute and forty-two seconds. At the end of treatment, S. walked from the session in one minute and thirty seconds. Walking both to and from the sessions improved during treatment. The rate of correct responses of matching numerals went from .75 to .80 correct responses per minute. Correct responses increased with treatment. Non-compliance was at 80% of all responses. At the end of treatment, non-compliance was reduced to 47% of all responses. S.'s non-compliant behavior was reduced significantly during treatment.

The greatest problem that S. has is in the area of social interaction and non-compliance. Future suggestions include more activities in which social interaction is emphasized. Walking must be included in all situations so that walking will become a behavior that will occur without prompting. S. enjoyed the movement to music activity and was most receptive to music with strong rhythm. Groups such as Chicago, Earth, Wind and Fire, the J. Geils Band and Michael Jackson worked very well. The non-compliant behavior that the client demonstrates could be reduced greatly if a program were implemented that would include the entire staff and all those that come in contact with S. Due to the improvement that S. has made with music therapy in this situation, I suggest that she take part in a music therapy program in the future.

____

Signature, MTS

Courtesy: Bill Brodginski

Final Evaluation and Recommendations: Music Therapy

May 3, 1985

Patient is a 70-y-o black female, diagnosed as having organic brain syndrome. My initial long term goals were to increase Pt's singing skills and to increase her social skills in relation to reality orientation. My music behavior objective was, Pt when verbally directed to "Sing *I'm looking Over a Four-Leaf Clover*," will sing the entire song for three consecutive sessions. My nonmusic behavior objective for Pt was, during the weekly group music therapy session, Mamie will independently praise and/or greet a neighbor for three consecutive sessions. I have completed a total of nine weekly group music therapy sessions with Pt. I have found Pt to be sedated on two occasions, causing her to be very tired. However, during the other sessions she has been one of the best participants. Not only has she sung *I'm Looking Over a Four-Leaf Clover* but many other songs, up to five in one half-hour session. She has stated that she enjoys music and our sessions. As far as greeting and praising a neighbor, she always does when told or asked to do so. Independently she has done so twice, which I feel is a major occurrence as she is visually impaired and cannot see who is around her.

My treatment has been to verbally praise her - "You sound better than ever today!" which causes her to laugh. I like to use this laughter as a reinforcer because we can share laughter, while she cannot see me to share a smile. I also use positive strokes on her arms and hands. My recommendation for this Pt is to continue in the weekly music therapy sessions. She not only sang, but also was toe-tapping and clapping, which could be increased in the future by another music therapist in a movement group in order to maintain motor skills.

Pt enjoyed sessions and even requested a song when asked if she had any favorites. Pt's favorite song is *I'm Looking Over a Four-Leaf Clover.*

____

Signature, MTS

Courtesy: Gail Ossman

Final Assessment

Pt is a 96-y-o Caucasian female diagnosed as having OBS, ASCVD, skin cancer and arthritis. Before treatment, Pt made no spontaneous statements and rarely imitated speech. She also had poor eye contact. Goals established for this client included increasing verbalization, increasing eye contact, increasing interactions with peers and performing a variety of rhythmic ostinati. Baseline data taken during the one-to-one music therapy session shows that Pt looked at the therapist for a mean level of performance at 58% over four sessions. It also shows that Pt vocalized the words to the chorus of *Home on the Range* at a mean level of 4.04%.

Treatment for the client consisted of contingent verbal praise, physical touch, smiling and singing *Goodnight, Irene,* when Pt vocalized a certain number of words. For looking at the therapist for 4 consecutive seconds, and for vocalizing any number of words to the chorus of *Home on the Range*, the therapist verbally and physically praised, as well as smiles at the client. If Pt vocalized five or more words to the chorus, the therapist sang *Goodnight, Irene*, a song that the client will sing along with while someone else is singing. Data on the music behavior during treatment shows that the mean number of words vocalized increased from 4.04% during baseline to 11.8% during treatment. Pt met the music objective which reads, "Given the verbal directive, 'Pt sing *Home on the Range*'", Pt will vocalize 10% of the total number of words to the chorus of the song for 4 consecutive sessions. Treatment data for the nonmusic behavior - maintaining eye contact - also taken during the individual music therapy session, shows that the percentage of times, Pt looked at the therapist for 4 consecutive seconds increased from a baseline mean of 58% to a treatment mean of 91.6%. Treatment data was gathered over six sessions. Although, the mean for the nonmusic behavior is high, Pt did not meet the objective which reads, "Given the verbal directive, 'Pt look at me,'" Pt will look at the therapist 85% of the times for 4 consecutive seconds for 4 consecutive sessions; however since during the last three sessions of treatment, Pt looked at the therapist for 4 seconds 100% of the times directed, it is projected that the behavior would have remained at a high enough rate so as to meet the objective and that if given one more session, Pt would meet the objective. Recommendations for future programming are as follows: 1) work on increasing spontaneous verbalizations; however it may be necessary to improve imitative speech first; 2) increase Pt's interactions with peers; 3) continue working on maintaining eye contact and increasing attention span. It is also suggested that the next therapist incorporate the song *Goodnight, Irene* as much as possible into the treatment session; Pt enjoys the song and sings and claps along with it.

____

Signature, MTS

Courtesy: Robyn Hurwitz

Final Evaluation and Recommendations: Music Therapy
May 3, 1985

Pt is a 30-y-o black male, diagnosed as having multiple sclerosis. My initial long term goals were to have Pt strum the portachord (a pressure-sensitive electronic music instrument) independently with his right hand. In conjunction with the music therapy sessions, I also planned to increase his coherent verbalization, as nods and gestures are a large portion of Pt's communication skills. My initial music behavior objective was, Pt during the one-to-one music therapy session will independently strum the portachord for two complete songs for three consecutive sessions. My initial nonmusic behavior objective was, during the one-to-one music therapy session, Pt will answer verbally (no nodding) three out of five questions, coherently, for three consecutive sessions. I have completed a total of ten one-to-one music therapy sessions with Pt. Data and graphs on Pt's behavior in relation to initial objectives show a definite increase of manual dexterity in Pt's right arm. Pt has been able to strum the portachord independently on several occasions. When Pt has not strummed independently, it has been due to his physical limitations (shaking involuntarily) and needs the slightest physical prompting on the therapist's part to guide Pt's hand. It is clearly evident by the graph on coherent verbalizations that Pt has surpassed my expectations and has even progressed to the point of initiating conversation.

The treatment program has been to praise, smile and touch Pt's arm or hand when he has completed a task. My recommendation for this Pt is to continue the one-to-one music therapy sessions, continuing also to use the portachord. Pt does, however, have certain physical limitations, as the M.S. has never gone into remission. This must be a consideration in the actual behavior portion of the future therapist's behavioral objective, because increasing a behavior may not be as realistic as maintaining a behavior which in this case is just as important.

Pt has enjoyed sessions and has progressed from a non-smiling, nodding person to actually laughing out loud in many sessions. Pt enjoys contemporary songs by artists such as Lionel Richie, Stevie Wonder, The Beatles and The Monkees. If possible, I feel that this program could make further strides if sessions could be held more than once per week.

____
Signature, MTS

Courtesy: Gail Ossman

APPENDIX: ADDITIONAL FORMS

The Repertoire Contract

Proficiency in accompanying singing, movement, instrumental, and listening activities is an essential skill for successful music therapy sessions. This form provides an outline for assessing such proficiency. The songs you learn this term should be interesting to the client and new to you. You must have the songs, accompaniments, and ostinati/activities memorized. (You should not glance at the music more than five times.) For example, if you are working with geriatric clients, learn popular songs from their younger years. If you are working with behavior disordered adolescents, learn current hits.

Repertoire Contract

	Name of Piece	Instrument	Date	Performance Evaluator and Grade
1.				
2.				
3.				
4.				
5.				
6.				
7.				
8.				
9.				
10.				
11.				
12.				
13.				
14.				
15.				

Grade Range:

5 = Performed very well, therapist glanced at music less than five times in three verses

4 = Performed well, therapist needed to look at music, rarely focused on client(s)

3 = Managed a simple piece, kept nose in music

2 = Muddled through, forgot melody/words/chords

1 = Desperately needs improvement

Performance evaluator should be instructor, peer, or music therapist on location. Instructor will grade at least three performances on location.

Peer/Self Observation Form

The Peer/Self Observation Form is intended to develop your ability to evaluate objectively your professional interaction with clients. In the final analysis, you can be your own best evaluator. Each of us needs to look at our work in order to acknowledge if our paperwork still coincides with our therapeutic procedures. There are many reasons why they may no longer coincide. These range from quick client progress, improved therapeutic skills, and/or personal feelings regarding the client. Also, we tend to judge our peers on the basis of peer interactions in addition to client interactions. The evaluations are often covert, not overt, and may be colored more by our feelings than behaviors we observe.

The form directs the student to ask either a peer of him/herself what the objectives and procedures are, and to observe and count the therapist and client behaviors. For a self observation, Items 1–14 should be completed. For a peer observation, Items 1 - 10 should be completed.

Peer/Self Observation Form

Music Therapy Practicum Date ______________

1. State desired client behaviors including in each the condition, behavior and criterion level.

   Music:

   Nonmusic:

2. If you are doing baseline/treatment (cross out what does not apply), what are:

   The number of music behaviors observed during the session _____________

   The number of nonmusic behaviors observed during the session _____________

3. State therapist's treatment behaviorally.

   Is the treatment procedure outlined being followed or has it been modified in some way?

   If is has been modified, state why (whether through inadvertence or intent - detail).

   If it has not been modified, do you think it should be modified? Why or why not?

   Is the definition or description of baseline or treatment procedure adequate to what is being done? Could this procedure be replicated by a stranger just from reading the description?

4. Is the client on any medication?______ If so, what is it? ________________________
   What is the dosage? _______________ What is its purpose? ______________________

   Typical side effects of this medication are:

   Does the client exhibit any of these? (Detail them.)

5. Take five minutes of the session and focus primarily on the therapist and count: Number of therapist smiles _________ Number of therapist approvals _______________.

6. Take five minutes of the session and focus primarily on the therapist and count: Number of client smiles _________ Number of client verbal approvals _______________.

7. List any noticeable deficits the client might exhibit in the following areas:

   Speech:

   Hearing:

   Display of Eye Contact:

   Fine Motor Coordination:

   Gross Motor Coordination:

   Following Instructions:

   Attention Span:

   Other:

8. What were the therapist music performance skills required for this activity?

   Were these performed competently or do they need improvement?

9. Was accompaniment accurate in terms of rhythm? ____________ tempi? ________________
   phrasing?____________ correct harmony? _____________ (Yes/Needs Improvement)

   Was musical leadership evident in terms of pitch entrance cues? ________________________
   rhythmic entrance cues? _____________________ rhythm? ________________________
   cut-off cues? ____________________ melody? __________________________
   ostinati? _____________________ phrasing? _____________________ (Yes/Needs Improvement)

10. Were the selections age-appropriate? ____________________

This section is to be completed as part of the self observation only.

11. If it was possible, would you prefer to have another client for this project? Why or why not?

12. Some clients one does not like. Is this one?________ If so, what behavior of the client is driving you up the wall?

13. After working with the client for _______ sessions, how important do you consider the behavior you initially decided to work on? ____Why?

    If there were to be ten more sessions, would you choose the same or other behaviors? Why?

14. As you consider the session, what made you feel really good about it?

Practical Suggestions for Running an Individual (1:1) Session

Sometimes it is desirable to work with a client individually. This would be the case when such individual work might benefit the client more than a group situation. For instance, a client's social behavior might be so maladaptive (hitting, biting, screaming) that to include him/her with other clients would disrupt the entire session (beyond any possible structure/control). Or, a client's skill level might be so low (rank beginner guitarist in a pop/rock combo) that including him/her in the group would set the stage for an unsuccessful music experience. Other clients may have needs that are truly unique (suicide attempts, eating disorders, teenage pregnancy), and may be best served in a 1:1 situation. In addition, some skills (instrumental) have traditionally been taught in individual sessions. When you decide that a client will be seen individually, be sure that it is for the client's benefit, and not just for yours (or anyone else's for that matter). With this in mind, let us assume that you have decided a 1:1 format will work best. Here are some suggestions to make your sessions function smoothly (and therapeutically):

To begin with, realize that working in a 1:1 situation may actually be **harder** than running a group. Why? The reason is simply that you have 100% of your attention to give your client, and therefore are expected to accomplish a lot more (data) than might be reasonably expected in a group setting (when you must attend to many clients at once). The behaviors you work with must be much more closely measured in the 1:1 session. In addition, you should plan to pinpoint, measure and treat at least several behaviors.

To accomplish this, consider these suggestions for collecting a wealth of information in your individual sessions:

1. Be sure that **you** as a student therapist are reinforcing to the client. It will only be you and him/her. If your client doesn't find you appealing enough to spend time with alone, you are back at square one.
2. Be careful that your 1:1 session is in an area that is easily accessible to other staff. If a problem (aggression, seizure) occurs, you want to be able to secure assistance **without** leaving the client alone.
3. If the client has a history of manipulative behavior, is a known liar, or has been involved in inappropriate sexual behavior (rape, promiscuity with staff), be sure that your session is **not** held behind closed doors, so if a client accuses you of trying something, you will be protected.
4. Don't "kill" a session by doing the same activity for too long. A thirty minute session might be divided in "mini-sessions" with varied activities. Remember, the client will not be getting the social stimulation found in a group setting.
5. Make sure to keep your approvals consistent and lively. Just because you are working 1:1 doesn't mean that your voice should be monotone or your face deadpan.
6. If your data collection procedures are noticed and questioned by your client, be honest with him/her. Explain to your client that you are writing things down to make sure you do a good job.

Often, your client will be modeling your social and musical behavior. Seeing you take data may motivate him/her to begin keeping records on progress/performance as well.

7. Be careful not to allow gaps to occur. Taking a lot of time to arrange materials, record data, or tune your autoharp (that's good for an entire session!) can provide a perfect opportunity for your client to go off-task.
8. Offer your client the opportunity to get a drink or use the bathroom **before** the session begins. These requests can serve as escape mechanisms during the session.
9. End each session with an activity that is enjoyable and easy for the client (listening to music, singing a favorite song). The session should end on an "up" note, so that the client looks forward to seeing you again.

Remember, in a 1:1 session your client will expect a lot from you. Be prepared to make sure his/her (as well as everyone else's) expectations are met!

Specific Considerations in Working with Clients in a Special Education Setting.

The inclusion of music therapy in special education settings has increased steadily since the passage of Public Law 94-142, The Education for All Handicapped Children Act of 1975. Music therapists have designed treatment programs geared specifically to the special education student. When working in such a setting it is important to take into account several considerations in order to make your work most effective.

To begin with, your students (students is the preferred term when working with clients in a school setting) will be in a state of transition. Whether you are working with a preschool, elementary, junior high (middle school) or high school student, you will need to take into account that your students will be in the special setting of in-between placement. Included in PL 94-142 is language which calls for the handicapped student to be educated in the least restrictive environment possible. This may mean that a student has been placed in a classroom from a more restrictive setting (a residential home for emotionally disturbed children) as a bridge to a public school mainstreamed classroom. Or, a student may have been placed in the present setting from a less restrictive setting because of failure in that setting (a retarded adolescent's falling far behind his/her normal peers in social, academic, and self-help skills). Regardless, your student will be in the special education setting only as long as is necessary to enable him/her to progress (or return) to a less restrictive (more normalized) setting.

Directly related to this transition factor is the fact that your students will need to develop specific skills to make that move towards the mainstream possible and successful. To contribute to this successful transition, you can help your students learn skills required for inclusion into the eventual mainstream. Social skills will be especially important, as disruptive or passive behavior often precludes a student's chance for success in a school setting. Music skills that can increase the chance for active participation in the mainstream are also important to assess and teach. These may range from identifying different styles of music from recordings to singing in tune or playing a band instrument.

Another important issue in working with children and adolescents is that of locus of stimulus control. A group of students can exert great influence over the behavior of each group member. "Peer pressure" is a reality in the classroom and can make or break the success of a therapy program. Often, you must plan carefully to ensure that you as a therapist can control and shape a group's behavior in light of competing stimuli (students). Try to have peer pressure work toward reinforcing desired behavior. Enlist the aid of your students and praise them for working toward the progress of the group as a whole. Group token contingencies can help structure activities so that each student behaves in a desired manner. After students have learned to act in a targeted manner, such prosthetic reinforcement procedures can be faded.

The therapist can also take advantage of the enormous stimulus control exhibited between students by having students model, record and praise behavior. Peer-tutoring and self-instruction can be effective in teaching students to become more independent in the classroom.

Finally, it is essential that you as a therapist are reinforcing to your student. Special education students are often in such settings because they have had problems functioning in regular classroom. Hence, "school" can be a frustrating environment, and adults can become associated with that frustration. If the student wants to work with, be like, and receive attention from you, your job as a therapist will be that much easier and successful.

Specific Considerations for Working with Clients in an Acute Care Setting

In an acute setting you mainly encounter clients between the ages of eighteen and sixty-five. The preferred term for such a client is patient, as the person is usually treated and released within a fairly short period (14 to 21 days). This is not to say that all acute patients successfully return to their previous situation. Some patients do not improve to the point of returning home and need long term (chronic) treatment.

With many acute-care patients, it is a recent event that has caused them to develop problems. These problems may range from depression and suicide attempts to agitation and excitability. Being a "patient" may be a new and frightening experience for these people. The therapist can help by establishing a positive relationship with the patient, who may feel alone. The patient may also need assistance in accepting the reality of his/her situation. Victims of accidents or catastrophes often deny that an event has taken place (a severe burn, amputation of a limb, loss of a loved one).

The music therapist must also consider how the patient interacts with other patients as well as with staff. The patient may have difficulty socializing and may not have a lot to say. Music activities can provide topics on conversation appropriate for "breaking the ice" with other patients.

Another consideration is that the patient may soon be returning to the environment associated with the identified problem. Thus, the patient can best be helped by teaching him/her skills to cope with that situation after being discharged.

Assessing, targeting skills and monitoring progress may seem impossible in an acute setting. Don't fall into the trap of using attendance as your sole category of data. Instead, measure and train behaviors that you can realistically monitor and assess in a short period of time. Skills such as verbal interaction, eye contact, positive statements about self, constructive use of leisure time, and relaxation to music are just some of the behavior areas that may be appropriate for intervention.

Often, patients can be taught to observe and record information concerning their progress. Procedures such as thought-stopping and the use of books for self-recording of data can be successfully trained in a short period of time.

Remember, many acute patients run the risk of becoming chronic patients if they are not taught new and successful ways to deal with their individual situations. You as a music therapist can help these patients recognize the reality of their situation and teach them ways to be happy and adapt once they are released.

Practical Considerations in Commonly Used Music Activities

Singing

Singing is one of those skills similar to roller skating, bicycle riding, and water skiing, once we learn how - there is no place like the shower. One may forget some words, but humming can never be ruled out. However, when we attempt to assess a client's music preference, we may run into a few problems. We certainly know what we like - and it becomes more obvious with the years - that our preferences determine what we spend our time listening to. A good modus operandi for ascertaining music preferences is to ask your client or his/her family. However, the question, "What should I ask?" comes immediately. (The problem here is often that the client may think that we want a specific answer and give us that answer rather than his/her real preferences.) If the patient says something like, "Oh anything," you can approach a more definite answer by thinking of music in terms of classes. The classes might be sacred, popular, classical, patriotic, seasonal, and folk (Irish, Spanish, American, etc.). This gives you a structure for seeking information. Among these general classes are many songs which we share in common. For popular songs, the *Sing Along With Mitch* series sometimes helps the therapist more than the patient. Other sources include records of Bing Crosby, folk singers, and Broadway musicals. One area of literature that is easy to miss in terms of preference is that of patients' children's preferences. Elvis' songs are often a big hit with older patients.

It is important to actually assess singing ability even with nonverbal clients. Patients with Alzheimer's disease who were no longer considered verbal have begun singing and talking to the therapist immediately following singing sessions. When we are assessing singing ability it is important to approve any efforts the client makes. In addition to typical approving remarks such as "good," "nice," "great," more specific comments encourage patient singing, e.g., "It helps when you hum with me," "It is reassuring for me to have you singing with me," "You remembered the words when I blanked out - great!" "Let me hear more!" Most of us even on our best days need encouragement to sing in front of others - our patients are no exception. Additionally, it is good to structure conversation in the session. A starting point is to ask three types of questions: yes/no, single word replies, and multiple answer responses. In terms of singing itself, it is important to allow the client's singing range to determine where the song will be sung, not the therapist's vocal range or this great new book we have (with all the songs in C). Many of the "golden oldies" do occur in books of this type. Never fear, this is not a major impediment to progress. Transposition comes to our rescue. This is a relatively simple process on a guitar, autoharp or other stringed instrument.

Listening

Listening is a more complex skill than is immediately apparent. Because listening occurs primarily in the dimension of time, there occur several competing forces which can occupy our attention. Witness our own infrequent daydreaming. In order to determine whether the client is listening or not, it is often necessary to conduct an informal operant listening assessment. This might consist of interrupting either songs from the patient's era or seasonal ones, and looking for any resulting physical movements. These might consist of turning/looking toward the previous sound source, crying/smiling, wiggling/lying still. As with singing, it is important to reinforce appropriate responses. This can be done verbally or tactilely. One consideration which has been found to be important with the profoundly retarded is the location of the sound source; I would suspect a parallel with certain geriatric patients as well. Dorow and Horton (1982) found that placing the sound stimulus by the patient's head increased response levels dramatically.

Following the initial assessment of response to music, it is necessary to provide some structure for listening. This may involve a verbal activity, a movement activity, or keeping a log of radio programs to which the client listens. There needs to be some overt client response to the music which allows us to assess reality orientation. For the low functioning client, this may involve having the therapist hold out his/her hands and the client tap a rhythm on them.

Instrumentation

Considerations of instrumental work involve the choice of an instrument itself, performance techniques, improvisation possibilities, and literature appropriate to skill development level. It may be easiest to begin with considerations of instruments and possible adaptations necessary for physically handicapped clients. Our experience has been that the most minimal adaptations are the best. The goal of the therapist in adapting an instrument or activity is to eliminate as many obstacles as possible; sometimes in creating a mechanical device to "aid" the client, we succeed in making the client more dependent. Adaptations can be designed to be either a temporary or a permanent means of performing the activity.

Temporary devices are any items which alleviate the initial problems a patient might encounter in learning a skill. They often include very simple items, e.g., a rubber thumb, a pencil with an eraser tip, an instrumental music stand, or velcro. (Of course, any of the above can also function as permanent devices.) A rubber thumb allows a patient with very sweaty fingers or a slight tremor to anchor his or her fingers on a keyboard instrument rather than to slide over several keys. The rubber tip of a pencil might also be used in this way. A music stand is handy for adjusting the height of hanging instruments, e.g., bells, triangle, tambourine, cymbals, gong, etc., allowing the client to drop them and also pick them up.

In terms of most permanent devices for the development of leisure time skills, the best adaptations are ones that the client can adjust and are inconspicuous. This may require the therapist to take an active role in directing the client toward activities in which he/she will be capable of attaining proficiency. With the severely involved this might include directing students toward a dulcimer rather than a guitar, or a harmonica rather than a more complex wind instrument. Adaptations can be of two basic types, either the client adapts the traditional technique used in playing an instrument of performing an activity, or the therapist provides a minimal additional device to allow the client to perform the activity. An example of the latter type is the Third Hand Capo. No matter the adaptation, close observation of the client's range and extent of motion and discussion with the client about how he/she might be able to perform the skill is important.

Improvisation

A basic consideration in improvisation in music is an atmosphere conducive to experimenting with tones and rhythms. Worrying is equivalent to spinning one's wheels in sand and the biggest obstacle we have towards "playing" with the basic elements of music. To encourage beginners to improvise, try using the pentatonic scale. It is a five-tone scale accredited to the ancient Greeks. It has no leading tones. This makes it ideal for beginners to learn improvisation (as the problematic areas of improvisation often lie with the leading tones). The pentatonic pattern corresponds to the five black keys on the piano. Frequently used pentatonic scales include: CDEGA, CDFGA, DEGAB and DEF#AB. Keys associated with these patterns include: C and G - CDEGA, C and F - CDFGA, G and D - DEBAG and D and A - DEF#AB. An association implies that if a piece of music is written in the key of C, for example, that pentatonic scale might be good for free melodic improvisation with that piece. After deciding on the tonality the therapist desires, he/she has the option of choosing from among several xylophone-like instruments which have removable tones. A major consideration in freeing the client to experiment is a definite rhythmic feeling and/or rhythmic pattern. Initially, it is best if the therapist sets the rhythmic pattern and the client develops a sense of his contribution to the ensemble.

Literature

The last area to discuss is that of literature. Following is a page for discussion of beginning points and the clients will hopefully have some suggestions. This listing of songs involves simplifications of chord arrangements in many cases.

Simplified Songs for Guitar, Ukulele, Autoharp, Tronichord and Omnichord

One Chord Songs: I

Row, Row, Row Your Boat
Frère Jacques
Have You Seen the Ghost of John
Shalom Chaverim
Three Blind Mice
There Was an Old Woman
Day is Done
The Farmer in the Dell
Hey, Ho, Nobody Home
Any Round

Two Chord Songs: I, V^7

Clementine
Crawdad Song
Down in the Valley
Hail, Hail, The Gang's All Here
He's Got the Whole World
Hush Little Baby
Jimmy Crack Corn
Old Texas
Old Chisolm Trail
Good News, Chariot-a-Comin'
Merrily We Roll Along
Rocka My Soul
Shoo, Fly, Don't Bother Me
Skip to My Lou
Swing Low, Sweet Chariot
Ten Little Indians
Tom Dooley
The More We Get Together
Yellow Submarine
Jacob's Ladder
The Old Grey Mare

Other Two Chord Songs

Oh, Sinner Man (a, G: e, D)
Drunken Sailor (a, G: e, D)
Old Joe Clark (D, C; A, G)

About the Third Hand Capo

The Third Hand Capo is a capo made of 6 rotating rubber discs. They allow the guitarist to clamp any string he/she desires. It also allows the client to play I, IV and V^7 chord in the key of E with only one finger. The address of the Third Hand Capo Company is: 716$^{1/2}$ West Lincoln Street, DeKalb, IL 60115.

The Third Hand Capo can also be used with the ukulele, banjo and mandolin. The company has published a guitar book for the capo entitled: the *Duck Soup Guitar Book*. It features 30 songs with very simple configurations.

About the Tronichord and Omnichord

The Tronichord and Omnichord are portable music computers similar to an autoharp. They come in several sizes (with prices to match), are manufactured by Suzuki.

Movement

Movement and music flow together. The ideas outlined below vary from freeform wheelchair dancing to disco dancing; one never knows how to get a client moving.

Freeform:

Freeform dancing as presented here requires one walker and one wheel chair ambulator. It would be recommended in two instances: 1) when the client cannot move his/her wheelchair, and 2) when the client is afraid to move his/her wheelchair in a social situation such as wheelchair dancing. The key to freeform dancing is the training of the volunteers or aides in interpreting the phrasing of the music so that the client feels that he/she is "dancing." Any style of dance music with obvious phrase lengths is appropriate; disco and folk dance tunes are recommended.

Disco:

Disco dancing as presented here requires one walker and one wheel chair ambulator with moderate to good movement possibility of the upper extremities. Specific movements include:

1. One-handed turn (underarm): Walker is to right of wheel chair ambulator moving parallel. W lifts W's left arm and guides WCA under W's left arm. (WCA moves backwards.)
2. Two-handed turn (underarm): W faces WCA. W walks backwards pulling WCA. W begins to turn WCA with both hands moving clockwise. They drop right hands and W pulls WCA round. They join hands.
3. Cross over and turn with one hand: W is on right side of WCA with hands crossed. They move parallel with WCA moving backwards while W goes forward. Both drop left hands and W guides WCA under W's right arm.
4. Promenade turn (crossed arms): W is on right side on WCA. Both move forward. W lifts right arm WCA under it.

Country Dancing:

Country dancing as presented here requires two wheel chair ambulators with moderate to good movement possibilities of the upper extremities. The obvious and (thank heaven) easy steps, such as "Everybody up and bow," and "Bow to your partner/corner," will not be discussed.

1. Swing: Clients move toward one another. Take hold of the closest arm of the partner's chair and wheel around with the other hand.
2. Chain: Clients move toward one another and reach out with the right hands to the other's right hand. They wheel with left hands as they move to opposite sides.
3. "Do-Si-Do" Clients move from opposite sides toward one another. They pass, going beyond so that they can make a "V" and back again passing or original place.
4. Promenade: Clients wheel parallel to partner in a circle.

Multiple Baseline Designs

A multiple baseline design allows the student therapist to observe and record several behaviors, clients or settings while beginning treatment with only one of these at a time. This is beneficial to both the student and the client(s), as it maximizes the use of techniques which have been deemed effective by the student. By observing a treatment's control (or lack of it) over a baseline, the student can determine when to begin applying the intervention to another baseline. This sequential approach helps the student "keep it all together" while continuously working with several baselines in a comprehensive approach.

There are three basic forms of multiple baseline designs. These are the multiple baseline across individuals (clients), across behaviors and across situations (settings) (Alberto and Troutman, 1986). Each will be discussed briefly as it relates to the practicum situation. The student interested in learning more about multiple baseline designs can consult a number of texts, including those by Hersen and Barlow (1976) and Kazdin (1982).

Multiple Baseline Across Clients

In this design, baseline data are collected on the same behavior of several clients. The absolute minimum number is two, but three or more are recommended. Choose a behavior that is likely to be emitted by the clients in your placement. Out-of-seat behavior would be good for behavior-disordered clients, while harmonica playing might not be. Out-of-seat behavior is common with this population (several or more clients). Harmonica playing is not as common, and it is unlikely that you could gather enough data (clients) to set up the design. Next, follow data collection and baseline procedures for the clients and the defined behavior. When the baselines of all clients are stable, begin treating one client, while continuing to collect data on the other clients. When the first client shows treatment effects, apply the treatment to another client. Continue this process until all clients are receiving the treatment. If a client does not respond to the intervention, then the treatment might be modified (B') as discussed in chapter IV. For the design to show that the treatment is controlling the behavior, data should show changes in slope or level at or near the point of intervention (change in phase).

Multiple Baseline Across Behaviors

This design would be appropriate for working in a 1:1 situation, where the student has the opportunity to carefully observe a single client (see Practical Suggestions for Running an Individual Session in the Appendix). Here several **independent** behaviors are observed, and treated sequentially, as in the above design. Select behaviors that you suspect will occur fairly frequently in the sessions. Observe the behaviors, and begin treatment with one after all show a stable baseline rate. As with the above design, two behaviors are a minimum, although three or more are recommended. As each behavior responds (graphically) to the treatment, apply the treatment to the next behavior.

Remember that you will be applying the same treatment to a number of differing behaviors. This makes the choices of behaviors and treatment very important. Powerful and concrete treatments (token contingencies, planned ignoring, prompting, contingent access to a reinforcer, etc.) are likely to be effective with a variety of behaviors (eye contact, smiling, in-seat, completion of math problems, etc.). As with the multiple baseline across clients, be sure that a behavior responds to treatment before proceeding to the next behavior. It is the sequential change in performance at or near the point of intervention that allows the student therapist to infer that the treatment has been responsible for changes in responding.

Multiple Baseline Across Settings

Here, a single behavior of a particular client is observed in a number of different settings of situations. As before, the minimum number of situations is two, although three or more is the recommended number. Select settings that the behavior is likely to occur in, and that are important to the client. For example, a multi-handicapped client's ability to lift him/herself out of a wheelchair and into a seat might be observed (and trained) in the classroom at the lunch table, in the bathroom at the toilet, and in the school bus. Another example might be an Alzheimer's patient's responding to his/her name being called by looking at the person in the hospital unit, on a walk on the hospital grounds, and in a shopping mall. These settings may seem so similar that sequential training may not seem necessary. However, small and seemingly insignificant changes in the environment often make transfer of training difficult for some clients. For instance, autistic clients may benefit from a multiple baseline across settings approach, as this population frequently does not generalize treatment effects across situations.

As with the other multiple baseline designs, begin by measuring and graphing data on the baselines (here, a single behavior of a particular client in a number of settings). When baselines are stable, begin the sequential application of treatment, waiting for each setting (baseline) to show change before treating the next setting.

Multiple-Probe Technique

One problem associated with multiple baseline designs can be the effects of repeated and extended baseline data collection. If a client cannot perform the behavior, or if access to other settings is not available, this collection may not be economical (Alberto & Troutman, 1986). Another undesirable situation may be a client's negative reaction be repeated testing, especially if he/she cannot perform the skill to be tested (Kazdin, 1982). A multiple-probe technique can allow the student therapist to observe behavior intermittently.

Graphing Data from Multiple Baseline Designs

The student should plot the data from each baseline using a separate axis for each dependent variable. This allows for visual inspection of changes in performance across baselines, as the intervention is applied in sequence. Below is a sample graph format (Alberto & Troutman, 1986).

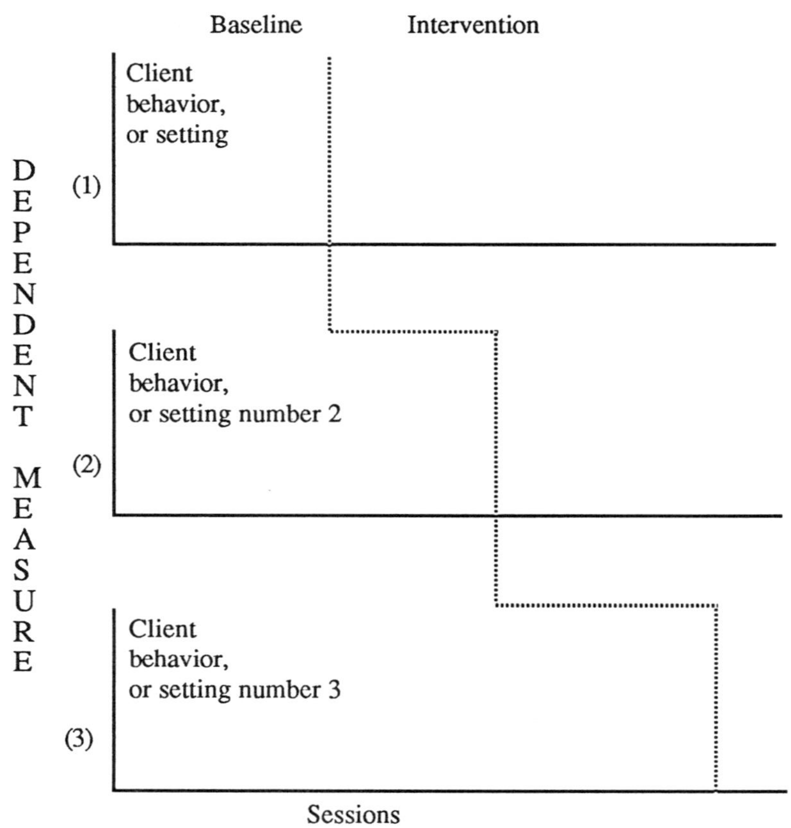

References

Alberto, P.A., & Troutman, A.C. *Applied behavior analysis for teachers* (2nd ed.). Columbus, OH: Merrill Publishing Co., 1986.

Bigge, J.L. *Teaching individuals with physical and multiple disabilities.* Columbus, OH: Merrill Publishing Co., 1982.

Dorow, L.G. & Horton, J.J. "Effect of the proximity of auditory stimuli and sung verses spoken stimuli on activity levels of severely/profoundly mentally retarded females." *Journal of music therapy*, 19 (1982), pp. 114-124.

Hersen, M.H., & Barlow, D.H. *Single-case experimental designs.* New York: Pergamon Press, 1976.

Iwata, B.A., Wong, S.E., Riordan, M. M., & Lau, M. M. "Assessment and training of clinical interviewing skills: analogue analysis and field replication." *Journal of applied behavior analysis*, 15 (1982), pp. 191-204.

Kazdin, A.E. *Single-case research designs: methods for clinical and applied settings.* New York: Oxford University Press, 1982.

Wheeler, A.L., & Fox, W.L. *Managing behavior: a teacher's guide to writing instructional objectives.* Lawrence, Kansas: H & H Enterprises, 1972.